SCHOLASTIC

Literary Passages:
Close Reading

Marcia Miller & Martin Lee

NEW YORK • TORONTO • LONDON • AUCKLAND • SYDNEY
MEXICO CITY • NEW DELHI • HONG KONG • BUENOS AIRES

Cover design: Tannaz Fassihi
Cover illustration: Patrick George
Interior design: Kathy Massaro
Interior illustrations by Doug Jones, Kelly Kennedy, Michael Moran, and Jason Robinson

ISBN: 978-0-545-79388-9
Copyright © 2016 by Scholastic Inc.
All rights reserved.
Printed in the U.S.A.
Published by Scholastic Inc.
First printing, January 2016.

1 2 3 4 5 6 7 8 9 10   40   23 22 21 20 19 18 17 16

Contents

Literary Text Passages

Character

Point of View

Setting/Mood

Key Events & Details

Sequence of Events

Conflict & Resolution

Context Clues

Compare & Contrast

Make Inferences

Summarize

Introduction

Reading, discussing, and sharing literary texts contributes greatly to the development of well-rounded minds. Exposure to diverse forms, characters, and plots set in varied time periods and cultures models for readers how the world works. Literary texts help us learn how people explore, interact, struggle, grow, and solve problems. In short, reading fiction enriches us!

Modern science supports that the human brain is hard-wired for stories. All cultures immerse their children in stories that explain the ways of the world while engaging their emotions. Although many students enjoy reading fiction, navigating the wide variety of rich literary texts poses challenges for evolving readers. Students may lack sufficient vocabulary or background knowledge to follow along. Some literary forms or features may be puzzling at first. This is why exposing students more frequently to complex literary texts and introducing them to active reading-comprehension strategies are now key components of successful reading instruction. Useful strategies, clearly taught, can empower readers to approach literary texts purposefully, closely, and independently. Such active tools provide students with a foundation for success not only in school, but for the rest of their lives.

> ### Connections to the Standards
>
> The chart on page 9 details how the lessons in this book will help your students meet the more rigorous demands of today's reading standards for literature.

Text Marking: A Powerful Active-Reading Strategy

To improve their comprehension of complex literary texts, students must actively engage with the material. Careful and consistent text marking by hand is one valuable way to accomplish this. To begin with, by numbering paragraphs, students can readily identify the location of useful narrative details when discussing a piece. By circling main characters, underlining pertinent clues to setting or sequence, and boxing key vocabulary, students interact directly with the material, making it more digestible in the process. But the true goal of teaching text marking is to help students internalize an effective close-reading strategy, not to have them show how many marks they can make on a page.

Purposeful text marking intensifies readers' focus. It helps them identify narrative elements as they read and recognize and isolate key details or connect relevant ideas presented in the text. For instance, boxing words like *first, then, next,* and *finally* can clarify the sequence of ideas or events in a passage. By underlining expressions like *the trouble is* or *one answer is*, students learn to identify conflicts and their resolutions. When students are asked to compare and contrast elements in a passage, boxing signal words and phrases, such as *both, but,* or *however,* can make identifying similarities and differences more apparent. Words like *since, because,* and *as a result* signal cause-and-effect relationships that structure a piece. Furthermore, the physical act of writing by hand, in itself, helps students not only process what they read, but remember it as well.

About the Passages

The 20 reproducible passages in this book, which vary by genre, form, purpose, tone, and task, address ten key reading-comprehension skills, from identifying character, point of view, setting, and key events and details, to sequencing, making inferences, and using context clues to unlock the meaning of unfamiliar words or phrases. Consult the Table of Contents to see the scope of skills, genres, forms, and Lexile scores of the passages. The Lexile scores fall within the ranges recommended for fifth graders. (The scores for grade 5, revised to reflect the more rigorous demands of today's higher standards, range from 830 to 1010. This range addresses the variety commonly seen in typical fifth grade classrooms.) *Note: The poem on page 46 does not include a Lexile score because poetry is excluded from Lexile measurements.*

Each passage appears on its own page, beginning with the title, the genre or form of the passage, and the main comprehension skill the passage addresses. All passages include illustrations. Some include common text elements, such as capital letters used for emphasis and captions.

The passages are stand-alone texts that can be used in any order you choose. Feel free to assign passages to individuals, pairs, small groups, or the entire class, as best suits your teaching style. However, it's a good idea to preview each passage before you assign it to ensure that your students have the skills needed to complete it successfully. (See the next page for a close-reading routine to model for students.)

Reading-Comprehension Question Pages

Following each passage is a reproducible "Do More" page of text-dependent comprehension questions: two are multiple-choice questions that call for a single response and a brief, text-based explanation to justify that choice. The other two questions are open-response items. The questions address a range of comprehension strategies and skills. All questions share the goal of ensuring that students engage in close reading of the text, grasp its key ideas, and provide text-based evidence to support their answers. Keep additional paper on hand so students have ample space to write complete and thorough answers.

Answer Key

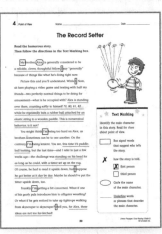

An Answer Key (pages 54–63) includes annotated versions of each marked passage and sample answers to its related questions. Maintain flexibility in assessing student responses, as some markings and answers to open-response questions may vary. (Because students are likely to mark different places in the text for particular skills, the annotated versions in the Answer Key highlight a variety of possible responses.) Encourage students to self-assess and revise their answers as you review the text markings together. This approach encourages discussion, comparison, extension, reinforcement, and correlation to other reading skills.

Teaching Routine for Close Reading and Purposeful Text Marking

Any text can become more accessible to readers who have learned to bring various strategies, such as purposeful text marking, to the reading process. Here is one suggested routine that may be effective in your classroom.

Preview

- **Engage prior knowledge** of the topic of the piece and its genre. Help students link it to similar topics or examples of the genre they may have read.

- **Identify the reading skill** for which students will be marking the text. Display or distribute the Comprehension Skill Summary Card that applies to the passage. Go over its key ideas. (See Comprehension Skill Summary Cards, pages 8, 10–12, for more.)

Model *(for the first passage, to familiarize students with the process)*

- **Display the passage** using an interactive whiteboard, document camera, or other resource, and provide students with their own copy. Preview the text with students by having them read the title and look at any illustrations or other graphic elements.

- **Draw attention to the markings** students will use to enhance their understanding of the piece. Link the text marking box to the Comprehension Skill Summary Card for clarification.

- **Read aloud the passage** as students follow along. Guide students to think about the skill and to write any questions they may have on sticky-notes.

- **Mark the text together.** Begin by numbering the paragraphs. Then discuss the choices you make when marking the text, demonstrating and explaining how the various text elements support the skill. Check that students understand how to mark the text using the various icons and graphics shown in the text marking box.

Read

- **Display the passage for a shared reading experience.** Do a quick-read of the passage together to familiarize students with it. Then read it together a second time, pausing as necessary to answer questions, draw connections, or clarify words as needed. Then read the passage once more, this time with an eye to the text features described in the text marking box.

- **Invite students to offer ideas for additional markings.** These might include noting unfamiliar vocabulary, an idiom or phrase they may not understand, or an especially interesting, unusual, or important detail they want to remember. Model how to use sticky-notes, colored pencils, highlighters, question marks, or check marks.

Respond

- **Have students read the passage independently.** This fourth reading is intended to allow students to mark the text themselves. It will also prepare them to discuss the piece and offer their views about it.

- **Have students answer the questions** on the companion Do More page. Depending on the abilities of your students, you might read aloud the questions to them, and then have them answer orally. Model how to look back at the text markings and other text evidence for assistance. This will help students provide complete and supported responses.

Comprehension Skill Summary Cards

To help students review the ten reading-comprehension skills this book addresses and the specific terms associated with each, have them use the ten reproducible Comprehension Skill Summary Cards (pages 10–12). The boldface terms on each card are the same ones students will identify as they mark the text.

You might duplicate, cut out, and distribute a particular Comprehension Skill Summary Card before assigning a passage that focuses on that skill. Discuss the elements of the skill together to ensure that students fully grasp it. Encourage students to save and collect the cards, which they can use as a set of reading aids whenever they read any type of literary text. Or display the cards in a reading center in your classroom that is available at all times.

Tips and Suggestions

- The text-marking process is versatile and adaptable. While numbering, boxing, circling, and underlining are the most common methods, you can personalize the strategy for your class if it helps augment the process. You might have students use letters or numbers to mark text; they can, for example, write MC to indicate a main character, D to mark a detail, or 1st for first-person point of view and 3rd for third-person. Whichever technique you use, encourage consistency of marking.

- You may wish to extend the text-marking strategy by having students identify other aspects of writing, such as figurative language or confusing words, expressions, or idioms. Moreover, you can invite students to write their own notes and questions in the margins.

Comprehension Skill

Character

Characters take part in the events of the story. A character can be a person, an animal, or a thing.

- Read for details that describe each character.
- Notice differences among characters so you can tell them apart.
- Notice whether and how a character changes or learns during the story.

A story may have a **main character** and one or more **minor characters**.

- The main character is the most important character in the story.
- A minor character is not the focus of the story.

Comprehension Skill

Point of View

Knowing *who* is telling a story gives you its **point of view**. What you learn in the story comes through that point of view. Authors usually use one of two points of view.

- **First-person** point of view has a character *in* the story telling it. In first-person stories, readers learn about events from that character's point of view. Look for words like *I*, *me*, and *we*.

- **Third-person** point of view has someone *outside* the story telling it. That person is the **narrator**. In third-person stories, readers learn the thoughts, actions, and feelings of many characters. Look for words like *he*, *she*, and *they*.

Comprehension Skill

Compare & Contrast

Authors often discuss people, places, things, or ideas by describing how they are alike and ways they differ.

- To **compare** means to tell how two or more things are alike.
- To **contrast** means to tell how two or more things are different.
- Comparing and contrasting help you understand a story's ideas, its plot, its characters, and its message.
- **Signal words** give clues that help you compare and contrast. (Examples for comparing: *both, too, like, also,* and *in the same way.* Examples for contrasting: *but, only, however, unlike,* and *different.*)

Literary Passages: Close Reading (Grade 5)
© Scholastic Inc.

Connections to the Standards

The lessons in this book support the College and Career Readiness Anchor Standards for Reading for students in grades K–12. These broad standards, which serve as the basis of many state standards, were developed to establish rigorous educational expectations with the goal of providing students nationwide with a quality education that prepares them for college and careers. The chart below details how the lessons align with specific reading standards for literary texts for students in grade 5.

These materials also address language standards, including skills in the conventions of standard English, knowledge of language, and vocabulary acquisition and use. In addition, students meet writing standards as they answer questions about the passages, demonstrating their ability to convey ideas coherently, clearly, and with support from the text.

Reading Standards for Literature	Passages
Key Ideas and Details	
Quote accurately from a text when explaining what the text says explicitly and when drawing inferences from the text.	1–20
Determine a theme of a story, drama, or poem from details in the text, including how characters in a story or drama respond to challenges or how the speaker in a poem reflects upon a topic; summarize the text.	1–20
Compare and contrast two or more characters, settings, or events in a story or drama, drawing on specific details in the text (e.g., how characters interact).	1–20
Craft and Structure	
Determine the meaning of words and phrases as they are used in a text, including figurative language such as metaphors and similes.	1–20
Explain how a series of chapters, scenes, or stanzas fit together to provide the overall structure of a particular story, drama, or poem.	1–3, 5–14, 16, 17, 19, 20
Describe how a narrator's or speaker's point of view influences how events are described.	1–4, 6–7, 9–11, 15, 17–18
Integration of Knowledge and Ideas	
Analyze how visual and multimedia elements contribute to the meaning, tone, or beauty of a text (e.g., graphic novel, multimedia presentation of fiction, folktale, myth, poem).	3–4, 6–11, 15, 17, 19
Compare and contrast stories in the same genre (e.g., mysteries or adventure stories) on their approaches to similar themes and topics.	2–5, 7–9, 11, 13–14, 18–20
Range of Reading and Level of Text Complexity	
By the end of the year, read and comprehend literature, including stories, dramas, and poetry, at the high end of the grades 4–5 text complexity band independently and proficiently.	1–20

Source: © Copyright 2010 National Governors Association Center for Best Practices and Council of Chief State School Officers. All rights reserved.

Character

Characters take part in the events of the story. A character can be a person, an animal, or a thing.

- Read for details that describe each character.
- Notice differences among characters so you can tell them apart.
- Notice whether and how a character changes or learns during the story.

A story may have a **main character** and one or more **minor characters**.

- The main character is the most important character in the story.
- A minor character is not the focus of the story.

Point of View

Knowing *who* is telling a story gives you its **point of view**. What you learn in the story comes through that point of view. Authors usually use one of two points of view.

- **First-person** point of view has a character *in* the story telling it. In first-person stories, readers learn about events from that character's point of view. Look for words like *I*, *me*, and *we*.
- **Third-person** point of view has someone *outside* the story telling it. That person is the **narrator**. In third-person stories, readers learn the thoughts, actions, and feelings of many characters. Look for words like *he*, *she*, and *they*.

Setting/Mood

The **setting** of a story tells *where* and *when* the story takes place. The setting can help create the **mood** or feeling of the story.

Read for details that tell where a story takes place.

- It can be a *real* place.
- It can be an *imaginary* place.

Read for details that tell when a story takes place.

- It might be set in the *present* (now).
- It might be set in the *past* (long ago).
- It might be set in the *future* (years from now).

Key Events & Details

Events are the actions or things that happen in a story. The events build interest and move the story along. But not all events have the same effect on the story.

As you read, think about which actions or things are **key events** and which are **details**.

- A key event is important to the theme or big idea of the story.
- Details tell more about a key event. Details may answer questions, such as *Who? Where? What? When? Why?* or *How?*

Literary Passages: Close Reading (Grade 5)
© Scholastic Inc.

Sequence of Events

In most stories, events happen in a certain order or **sequence**. Some events happen in the *beginning* of the story. Other things happen in the *middle*. The story finishes with events that happen at the *end*.

- As you read, think about the sequence of events. This helps you follow the story. Picture the events in your mind to help you remember the sequence.

- **Signal words** give clues about the sequence of events. (Examples: *before, first, second, next, then, now, later, after,* and *finally*; as well as specific dates and times.)

Conflict & Resolution

Good stories have a **plot**. The plot is the set of key events that move the story along. Most stories present a problem and how it gets solved. This relationship is called **conflict and resolution**.

- A conflict is a form of trouble, problem, or disagreement.

- A resolution is the way the conflict gets solved.

- **Signal words** are clues to a conflict and its resolution. (Examples for conflicts: *question, challenge, dilemma, puzzle, need,* and *trouble*. Examples for resolutions: *answer, result, idea, plan, reason, solution, solve, improve,* and *fix*.)

Context Clues

Authors may use words you may not know. But nearby words or sentences can offer clues about the meaning of an unknown word.

- **Context** refers to all the words and sentences around an unknown word.

- **Context clues** are hints that can help you figure out a word's meaning. As you read, search for related words, such as synonyms, antonyms, explanations, or examples in nearby text. Link these clues to the unknown word to understand it.

Compare & Contrast

Authors often discuss people, places, things, or ideas by describing how they are alike and ways they differ.

- To **compare** means to tell how two or more things are alike.

- To **contrast** means to tell how two or more things are different.

- Comparing and contrasting help you understand a story's ideas, its plot, its characters, and its message.

- **Signal words** give clues that help you compare and contrast. (Examples for comparing: *both, too, like, also,* and *in the same way.* Examples for contrasting: *but, only, however, unlike,* and *different*.)

Literary Passages: Close Reading (Grade 5)
© Scholastic Inc.

Make Inferences

Authors may hint at an idea without stating it directly. But they usually include enough detail so readers can use what they already know about a topic to "read between the lines" and figure out a hidden message.

- **Text clues** are words or details that help you figure out an unstated idea.

- You **make an inference** by combining text clues with what you already know to form a likely conclusion, or "educated guess."

Summarize

As you read, check that you understand and can recall the key elements of a story. Think about how to retell the important parts in your own words. Leave out minor details and get to the point.

- The **topic** or **theme** of a story is its focus—what it is mainly about.

- **Key details** add more information and support the story's theme.

- A **summary** briefly restates the theme using only the key details. A good summary is short, clear, and tells only what is most important.

Literary Passages: Close Reading (Grade 5)
© Scholastic Inc.

Literary
Text Passages

Fishing With Grandpa Leon

Read the realistic fiction.

Then follow the directions in the Text Marking box.

Ronan was beside himself with excitement. He was ten years old and his Grandpa Leon was finally going to take him fishing. Grandpa Leon claimed to be "a fishing expert, practically a professional angler." He told Ronan that he'd caught giant marlin and huge tuna, and that he had many adventurous stories to tell. He promised he'd supply all the fishing gear: rods, reels, hooks, bait, buckets, and plenty of food, too. All Ronan had to do was to be ready promptly at 6 AM.

As it happened, it was good Grandpa Leon brought plenty of food because grandfather and grandson had plenty of time to eat it. The fish simply weren't biting. "They're napping," he informed Ronan, knowingly.

No nibbles left plenty of time for Grandpa Leon's elaborate fish stories. In fact, it was during one of those tall tales that Ronan suddenly felt a sharp tug on his line. "I've got something really huge!" he shouted.

"Hold tight, I'll help," Grandpa Leon replied, reaching over and grabbing the rod. Together, they tugged on the line that held what promised to be a colossal, prize-winning fish. Finally, they reeled in their catch—a tattered leather suitcase, heavy with sand.

"How about that, Ronan—the first suitcase of the day!" Grandpa Leon exclaimed, adding, "You can't say it wasn't a big catch!"

Text Marking

Identify the characters in the story.

⬭   Circle the 2 characters.

___   Underline some details about each character.

Name _____ Date _____

Fishing With Grandpa Leon

▶ **Answer each question. Give details from the realistic story.**

1 Which best describes what *anglers* do?

  ◯ A. They tell stories.   ◯ C. They draw angles.

  ◯ B. They supply food.   ◯ D. They fish with rods and reels.

What helped you answer? _____

_____

_____

2 Which best describes Grandpa Leon?

  ◯ A. He is confident and cheerful.   ◯ C. He is very famous.

  ◯ B. He is cranky and strict.   ◯ D. He doesn't like to joke around.

What helped you answer? _____

_____

_____

3 Summarize the fishing experience, as seen through Ronan's eyes.

_____

_____

_____

_____

_____

_____

4 What was surprising about Grandpa Leon's reaction to catching a suitcase?

_____

_____

_____

_____

_____

Literary Passages: Close Reading (Grade 5)
© Scholastic Inc.

Name _____ Date _____

A Cabin in Syracuse, 1855

Read the historical fiction.

Then follow the directions in the Text Marking box.

In the years before the Civil War, some concerned citizens teamed up to assist runaway slaves in their perilous effort to escape bondage. They formed a network of safe houses along the routes north. Elijah's cabin in Syracuse, New York, was part of this Underground Railroad.

One blustery winter night, the family awoke to frantic rapping at the door. Elijah opened it to see Amos, a friend from nearby Manlius, with two runaways—a young woman and a small girl, both looking terrified and both shivering in drenched, tattered clothes.

"Come, sit by our fire," said Elijah's mother, who was welcoming. "I'll have Elijah get it roaring again, and then I'll find you some dry clothes and warm food."

"Oh, thank you kindly, ma'am," replied the woman as the two runaways entered. "I'm Nola, and we've been running hard for days. My little Ruby here is powerful hungry."

Meanwhile, Elijah listened carefully to his instructions from Amos. "You'll keep them here two days," he said gravely. "Best get your hiding space ready, as slave catchers have been spotted nearby."

Flashing two fingers to signal his mother, Elijah then sat with the guests as they ate and drank heartily. *How long had it been since their last meal,* he wondered. Whiskers trotted over to meet the strangers. Ruby timidly stroked the furry cat and smiled—possibly for the first time in days.

Text Marking

Identify who the story is about.

◯ Circle the main character.

▭ Box the other characters.

_____ Underline details about each character.

Literary Passages: Close Reading (Grade 5)
© Scholastic Inc.

Name _____   Date _____

A Cabin in Syracuse, 1855

▶ **Answer each question. Give details from the historical fiction.**

1 Who is telling this story?

○ A. Amos   ○ B. Elijah   ○ C. Elijah's mother   ○ D. a narrator

What helped you answer? _____

_____

_____

2 Which is a synonym for *bondage*?

○ A. employment   ○ B. slavery   ○ C. starvation   ○ D. freedom

What helped you answer? _____

_____

_____

3 Make inferences using details from the story. What kind of person is Elijah?

_____

_____

_____

_____

_____

_____

_____

4 What is the purpose of the opening paragraph?

_____

_____

_____

_____

_____

_____

The Expedition

Read the adventure story.
Then follow the directions in the Text Marking box.

They'd been trapped by ice for 36 days and had been on their own for longer than that, ever since a storm separated them from the ship and the rest of the crew on their expedition. Karl was in a pitiful state—lost, weak, frightened, and shivering from unrelenting cold. He was also suffering the painful effects of frostbite.

Suddenly, ice cracked enough for the boat to break loose and begin to bob gently in the frigid sea. The crew cheered their good fortune. No longer stuck in the ice, their chances of survival had edged up a notch. But Karl understood that the struggles had not ended, as medical supplies were nearly gone and there was barely any food left. If that weren't terrifying enough, the maps were lost, too.

The crew navigated icy waters until their hands bled and muscles ached. For days, Karl saw nothing in the muted, constant light but other ice floes. Then, finally, he detected a sound in the stillness that he hadn't heard for months: the cawing of birds. That sweet sound signaled that land was near. All were exhilarated!

The land they found was snow-covered and flat. The crew rowed along its barren coast until they spotted the mouth of a river. Karl and the men entered, presuming it would lead to a village and safety. On they plodded, ever more hopeful of survival.

Text Marking

Identify who is telling this story.

☐ Box signal words that suggest who tells the story.

X how the story is told.

☐ first person

☐ third person

_____ Underline words or phrases that tell about Karl.

The Expedition

▶ **Answer each question. Give details from the story.**

1   Which best states the theme of this story?

○ A. Boating   ○ B. Nature   ○ C. Survival   ○ D. Weather

What helped you answer? _____

_____

_____

2   Which word can replace *unrelenting* in the first paragraph without changing its meaning?

○ A. constant   ○ B. freezing   ○ C. pitiful   ○ D. terrifying

What helped you answer? _____

_____

_____

3   In paragraph 2, the narrator says "…their chances of survival had edged up a notch." Why was the narrator not more enthusiastic at the moment?

_____

_____

_____

_____

_____

4   Based on the details of this story, describe where you think it takes place.

_____

_____

_____

_____

_____

_____

Literary Passages: Close Reading (Grade 5)
© Scholastic Inc.

The Record Setter

Read the humorous story.
Then follow the directions in the Text Marking box.

My brother, Alex, is generally considered to be a reliable, clever, thoughtful fellow. I say "generally" because of things like what he's doing right now.

Picture this and you'll understand. While I, Nate, sit here playing a video game and texting with half my friends—two perfectly normal things to be doing for amusement—what is he occupied with? Alex is standing over there, counting softly to himself *79, 80, 81, 82…* while he repeatedly bats a rubber ball attached by an elastic string to a wooden paddle. This is nonsensical behavior, is it not?

You might think I'm being too hard on Alex, as brothers sometimes can be to one another. On the contrary, I'm being lenient. You see, this time it's paddle-ball batting, but the last time—and I refer to just a few weeks ago—the challenge was standing on his head for as long as he could, with a timer set up on the rug. Of course, he had to read it upside down, but I suppose he got better at it day by day. Maybe he should've put the timer upside down, too.

Frankly, I'm getting a bit concerned. What if one of his goofy pals introduces him to alligator wrestling? Or what if he gets enticed to take up tightrope walking from skyscraper to skyscraper? I tell you, for Alex, these ideas are not too far-fetched!

Text Marking

Identify the main character in this story. Read for clues about point of view.

☐ Box signal words that suggest who tells the story.

✗ how the story is told.
   ☐ first person
   ☐ third person

◯ Circle the name of the main character.

___ Underline words or phrases that describe the main character.

Literary Passages: Close Reading (Grade 5)
© Scholastic Inc.

Name _____ Date _____

The Record Setter

▶ **Answer each question. Give details from the humorous story.**

1   To amuse himself, Nate likes to…

    ○ A. …wrestle alligators.   ○ C. …play table tennis.

    ○ B. …praise his brother.   ○ D. …play video games.

What helped you answer? _____

_____

_____

2   Which is a synonym for *lenient*?

    ○ A. easygoing   ○ B. critical   ○ C. loving   ○ D. harsh

What helped you answer? _____

_____

_____

3   How does Nate use exaggeration to get across his point about his brother's behavior?

_____

_____

_____

_____

_____

_____

4   Imagine Alex describing Nate. How might the story be different?

_____

_____

_____

_____

_____

_____

_____

_____

Literary Passages: Close Reading (Grade 5)
© Scholastic Inc.

Name _____ Date _____

The Beach House

Read the suspense story.
Then follow the directions in the Text Marking box.

The water was glistening in the summer's morning sunlight and the surf was cool on their feet as Krin and Paula happily strolled along the water's edge. Collecting shells and skimming stones as they went, the brother and sister were having a ball exploring what appeared to be a never-ending beach.

After a while, they stopped and looked back. Their parents and the umbrellas, chairs, and crowds were a long way off. But just ahead, nestled amongst sea grape trees, stood a run-down house. It appeared to be unoccupied; curious, they went to investigate.

The steps creaked as they ascended them, as did the porch when they stepped onto it. The shutters and porch railing were weathered and broken. The front door was ajar so they squeezed through and cautiously entered. The place was in total disarray, chockablock with dust, sand, dead leaves, and overturned, splintered furniture. They'd taken but a few steps when the door unexpectedly slammed shut behind them.

Startled, Krin and Paula spun around. Before they could even utter something like "Uh-oh," the window shutters clapped closed, too. And if this wasn't scary enough, the stairs to the second floor squeaked. When a light in the back bedroom flickered, that was absolutely the final straw.

"Let's get outta here, Paula!" And out they ran, all the way back to those wonderful umbrellas, beach chairs, and crowds.

Text Marking

Think about the setting and mood of the story.

☐ Box **WHEN** it takes place.

✗ **WHEN** the story is set.

☐ past

☐ present

☐ future

⬭ Circle **WHERE** it takes place.

_____ Underline details that set the mood.

Literary Passages: Close Reading (Grade 5)
© Scholastic Inc.

Name _____ Date _____

The Beach House

▶ Answer each question. Give details from the suspense story.

1 Who is telling the story?

○ A. Krin   ○ B. Paula   ○ C. a narrator   ○ D. a ghost

What helped you answer? _____

_____

_____

2 Things that are *chockablock* are _____.

○ A. full of blocks   ○ B. crowded together   ○ C. run-down   ○ D. broken

What helped you answer? _____

_____

_____

3 Why did Krin and Paula end up viewing the crowded beach as *wonderful*?

_____

_____

_____

_____

_____

_____

_____

4 Summarize the setting and moods of the story. How does the mood change?

_____

_____

_____

_____

_____

_____

_____

_____

Literary Passages: Close Reading (Grade 5)
© Scholastic Inc.

Name _____   Date _____

Mile-and-a-Quarter Monkey

Read the descriptive story.
Then follow the directions in the Text Marking box.

It had taken us nearly five hours from the river to reach Three-Mile House that hot summer day in the Grand Canyon. We were already tiring from the hike, and knowing that a relentlessly uphill slog still lay ahead, we gratefully rested there.

The trail wound upward through awesome—in the true sense of the word—scenery, rich with spectacular rock formations. The other hikers in the hut, also fatigued from their challenging climbs, seemed in an upbeat mood. Eventually, we gathered our courage to resume the twisting trail to the rim.

Mile-and-a-Half House was our next stopping point, and reaching it was a steady struggle. Our muscles ached, our gusto was diminished, and we were drained upon arrival. After a much-appreciated second rest, longer than our first, we reluctantly began the final leg of our ascent.

The hike was not getting any easier in the heat, and we paused continuously. While wishing the trek were over, we spotted it overhead: an immense monkey face! That's precisely what the eroded rocks looked like. We excitedly told everyone we passed about where to see Mile-and-a-Quarter Monkey, as we named it. Each hiker gladly promised to keep a lookout for it. Suddenly, amazingly, we felt a renewed bounce in our step. Discovering the giant monkey face had put wings on our feet. Energized, we practically flew out of the canyon, and that was awesome, too.

Text Marking

Think about the setting and mood of the story.

☐ Box WHEN it takes place.

◯ Circle WHERE it takes place.

✗ the setting.
  ☐ realistic
  ☐ imaginary

___ Underline details that set the mood.

Mile-and-a-Quarter Monkey

▶ **Answer each question. Give details from the story.**

1 What best describes the mood of the hikers as they approached their second rest stop?

○ A. bored and miserable   ○ C. exhausted and a little grumpy

○ B. gloomy and disappointed   ○ D. cheerful and full of anticipation

What helped you answer? _____

_____

_____

2 Which would be a *trek*?

○ A. a car ride to the mall   ○ C. a skateboard ride down a hill

○ B. a lengthy hike in the snow   ○ D. a relaxing stroll around the block

What helped you answer? _____

_____

_____

3 What factors made the hike so challenging?

_____

_____

_____

_____

_____

4 Explain the reason for the hikers' change in mood on the final leg of their ascent.

_____

_____

_____

_____

_____

_____

Literary Passages: Close Reading (Grade 5)
© Scholastic Inc.

Medieval Festival

Read the fantasy.
Then follow the directions in the Text Marking box.

Driving to the Medieval Festival, Mom sang old folksongs while Gavin studied the long list of events. There would be sword classes, blacksmithing, acrobats, dancers, jesters, and more, but it was jousting that was his top priority.

When the two entered the festival grounds, a whirl of sights, sounds, and smells overwhelmed them. Sheep and goats grazed beside horses and mules. The scent of fresh cider perfumed the air while strolling jugglers and musicians entertained the crowds. As Gavin pulled Mom toward the jousting field, he was so busy gawking that he tripped and fell. When he arose, his mother was gone and his body felt unusually heavy. Yikes! He was wearing a full suit of armor!

Text Marking

Think about the key events in Gavin's experience.

◯ Circle at least 3 key events.

_____ Underline details about each event.

"Sir, your steed awaits!" announced a man in a cloak, directing Gavin toward the stable. Too stunned to protest, Gavin clanked along, huffing under the armor's weight.

"I think you're mistaken," Gavin sputtered.

"Not so!" replied the squire. "Queen Mab commands you to replace Sir Harry, who broke his arm yesterday. Ride proudly to honor her!"

Gavin gulped, feeling equally confused and thrilled at this crazy turn of events. He'd wanted to see a joust, but to actually participate in one? Zounds!

The squire paraded Gavin and his horse into position and handed him the long pole. Across the field was his fierce opponent, fully armored and ready...

Name _____ Date _____

Medieval Festival

▶ **Answer each question. Give details from the fantasy.**

1 What is the main purpose of a Medieval Festival?

○ A. It is a great place to drink cider.

○ B. It allows visitors to see farm animals up close.

○ C. It lets people experience medieval events and activities.

○ D. It provides a chance for people to practice battle skills.

What helped you answer? _____

_____

_____

2 Which means nearly the same as *gawking*?

○ A. staring　　○ B. juggling　　○ C. thinking　　○ D. strolling

What helped you answer? _____

_____

_____

3 This story seems to take place in two settings and times. Explain this.

_____

_____

_____

_____

_____

4 Make an inference to explain Gavin's mixed feelings upon finding himself a knight about to joust.

_____

_____

_____

_____

_____

Name _____ Date _____

Block Party Celebrity

Read the community story.
Then follow the directions in the Text Marking box.

Newly moved in and eager to meet their neighbors, the Guerrero family had a great idea. They would serve Rosa's delicious *elote*, a favorite savory dip made with corn and cheese, at the block party.

They set up their table in front of their house, located at the quiet end of the block, far from the busy avenue. The family was in a jovial mood as they set up aluminum trays of *elote*, tortilla chips, plastic bowls, forks, and napkins.

Despite the appealing aroma of corn, few people strolled over, distracted by temptations elsewhere on the block. With few neighbors to serve, Ms. Guerrero permitted Yimi and Luisa to explore. When they returned, ice creams in hand, a commotion grabbed their attention. It was the town's mayor, Elena Carillo-Lopez, and her entourage. They had arrived at the Guerrero's end of the block.

The mayor stopped first at their table, smiling warmly as Luisa heaped *elote* into a bowl, added some chips, a fork, and served it with a napkin.

"Holy *guacamole*, your *elote* is the best!" the mayor exclaimed, glowing with each mouthful.

Rosa blushed, saying, "*Gracias, señora.*"

Well, that did it. It seemed now that everybody else made a bee-line to the Guerrero table for *elote*. They were newcomers no longer.

Text Marking

Think about the key events of the story.

◯ Circle 4 main events in the story.

_____ Underline details about each event.

Literary Passages: Close Reading (Grade 5)
© Scholastic Inc.

Name _____   Date _____

Block Party Celebrity

▶ **Answer each question. Give details from the community story.**

1 Why did the Guerreros set up a table at the block party?

○ A. They wanted to meet the mayor.

○ B. They wanted to open a restaurant.

○ C. Their house was located at the end of the block.

○ D. They hoped the block party would help them meet their neighbors.

What helped you answer? _____

_____

_____

2 What happened after the mayor tasted the *elote*?

○ A. Ms. Guerrero voted for the mayor.   ○ C. The children finished their ice creams.

○ B. Many others came over to try it.   ○ D. The mayor left to get a beverage to wash it down.

What helped you answer? _____

_____

_____

3 What caused the Guerreros to no longer feel like newcomers?

_____

_____

_____

_____

_____

4 Explain the meaning of the title. Who is the celebrity at the block party?

_____

_____

_____

_____

_____

Literary Passages: Close Reading (Grade 5)
© Scholastic Inc.

Painted Sneakers

Read the crafts story.
Then follow the directions in the Text Marking box.

Packing my van by 7 AM gives me time to get to the lake for this autumn's crafts market. The winding drive will be lovely, as will the reunions with my fellow craftspeople, folks I see once a year.

Before coffee and chit-chat, I set up my booth. First, I assemble the lightweight aluminum poles that frame my protective canopy. After all, the market takes place come rain or shine. Then I set up my tables and racks to hold my one-of-a-kind, hand-painted sneakers. I put my most popular superhero and cartoon pairs on racks so their designs attract customers. Next, I set out other items—wild laces, goofy flip-flops, hair ornaments—neatly in trays. After that, I set out an album showing all my designs for customers to flip through, and a sign-up book for people who want to get on my mailing list.

Customers start arriving by 11 AM, so everything must be ready. My last task is to activate and test my wi-fi payment machine so I can accept cash and credit cards. At that point, my sneakers and I are prepared for the market to open.

I stand most of the day—wearing my favorite sneakers—but rarely feel tired. Most shoppers are friendly and curious, which encourages me to tell more about my work. Occasionally, I slip away for a quick snack. Once in a while, I even sit down…! At 6 PM, when the market closes, I pack, load my van, and return home.

Text Marking

Mark the sequence of events in the story.

☐   Box at least 7 signal words about sequence and time.

_____   <u>Underline</u> some key events in the painter's day.

1-2-3-4-5   Number the events in order.

Name _____ Date _____

Painted Sneakers

▶ **Answer each question. Give details from the crafts story.**

1 Who is telling this story?

○ A. a narrator   ○ B. a reporter   ○ C. the painter   ○ D. a customer

What helped you answer? _____

_____

_____

2 Which statement best captures the meaning of *come rain or shine*?

○ A. Weather is difficult to predict.   ○ C. It takes rain and shine for crops to grow.

○ B. The event will happen in any weather.   ○ D. It never snows in that part of the country.

What helped you answer? _____

_____

_____

3 In what ways are the beginning and the end of day similar for the craftsperson?

_____

_____

_____

_____

_____

_____

4 Make an inference. Think about the events the sneaker painter describes.
About when would you expect this person to get home? Explain.

_____

_____

_____

_____

_____

_____

Literary Passages: Close Reading (Grade 5)
© Scholastic Inc.

Name _____ Date _____

The Relief Pitcher

Read the sports story.
Then follow the directions in the Text Marking box.

Wilson is clearly in trouble—he has walked two batters in a row, has been taking too much time between pitches, and looks weary. Recognizing this, the team's manager and pitching coach exchange worried glances and confer softly. The coach picks up the phone in the dugout to call the bullpen coach, step 1 in the relief-pitching process.

Next, there is action in the bullpen behind left field. Two pitchers, a righty and a lefty, get up. After doing a series of gentle stretches, each hurler grabs his glove, stands on a mound, and begins to toss the ball softly to his catcher. After briefly warming up, both relievers start throwing harder, expecting that one of them will likely be called into the game.

Then there is more trouble for Wilson. Another walk draws the manager from his perch by the dugout railing. He's had enough. On his way to the mound, he waves his left hand, signaling the bullpen. Seeing this, the lefty stops throwing, opens the bullpen gate, and jogs to the mound to replace Wilson.

When the manager reaches the mound, he takes the ball from the struggling pitcher, who leaves the field with his head down. Next, the manager greets the incoming reliever, and gives him the ball and some encouragement. Finished, the manager trots back to the dugout, hoping he's made the right choice.

Text Marking

Mark the sequence of events in the story.

☐ Box at least 7 signal words about sequence and time.

_____ Underline some key events.

1-2-3-4... Number the events in order.

Literary Passages: Close Reading (Grade 5)
© Scholastic Inc.

Name _____ Date _____

The Relief Pitcher

▶ **Answer each question. Give details from the sports story.**

1 What is the manager's first step in the process of relieving his struggling pitcher?

○ A. He has the coach call the bullpen to get pitchers warming up.

○ B. He begins tossing the ball softly.

○ C. He walks another batter.

○ D. He walks to the mound.

What helped you answer? _____

_____

_____

2 Why are the manager and coach concerned?

○ A. It is raining.   ○ C. There is action in the bullpen.

○ B. They don't know what to do.   ○ D. They think that their pitcher is tiring.

What helped you answer? _____

_____

_____

3 Make an inference about the narrator of this baseball story?

_____

_____

_____

_____

_____

4 Summarize the events in this story, focusing on the conflict and its possible resolution.

_____

_____

_____

_____

_____

_____

Literary Passages: Close Reading (Grade 5)
© Scholastic Inc.

Name _____ Date _____

Krishna's Lesson

Read the legend from India.
Then follow the directions in the Text Marking box.

Though small and gentle, young Krishna had great wisdom bestowed upon him by Lord Vishnu. In those days, Krishna lived in Vrindavan. Each year, the people there made offerings to Indra, the fierce ruler of clouds and rain, hoping to soothe Indra's temper. Krishna clearly recognized that Indra was neither generous nor sincere; he was selfish and arrogant, unworthy of respect.

To teach Indra a lesson, Krishna addressed the people. "Indra is a bully we need not serve. Instead, it makes more sense to worship Govardhan, our mountain that supports us. Let us honor kind Govardhan, who selflessly shares her lush forests and urges the clouds to shower us." The people approved Krishna's solution.

Indra flew into a mighty rage. "These farmers ignore *me* to worship a mountain on the advice of a child? I shall severely punish this insult," he thundered. Indra ordered the clouds to send furious winds and driving rains to Vrindavan. The tempest terrified the people, who fearfully sought help from young Krishna.

With supreme calm, grace, and power, Krishna lifted Govardhan into the air using only the little finger of his left hand. He steadfastly held the mountain like an umbrella, protecting Vrindavan for seven stormy days and nights.

Finally, Indra acknowledged his error. He halted the storm and deeply apologized to Krishna. Thus did humans learn not to give in to disaster.

Text Marking

The story describes a problem. Identify it and read for how it gets solved.

[ ] Box these signal words: **temper, solution, apologized**

[ ] Box the conflict.

_____ Underline the resolution.

( ) Circle details about Krishna.

Name _____ Date _____

Krishna's Lesson

▶ **Answer each question. Give details from the legend.**

1 Which term best describes the personality of Indra?

○ A. generous   ○ B. graceful   ○ C. terrorizing   ○ D. respectful

What helped you answer? _____

_____

_____

2 According to the legend, Vrindavan is _____.

○ A. a god   ○ B. a mountain   ○ C. a ruler   ○ D. a village

What helped you answer? _____

_____

_____

3 Why did it take Krishna's help to convince the people to stop honoring Indra?

_____

_____

_____

_____

_____

_____

4 How does the legend make clear that Krishna was wise and honorable?

_____

_____

_____

_____

_____

_____

_____

Literary Passages: Close Reading (Grade 5)
© Scholastic Inc.

Talent Show Contest

Read the entertainment story.
Then follow the directions in the Text Marking box.

Ms. Spira, the music teacher, was nearly finished auditioning hopefuls for the upcoming talent show. She announced to the two remaining candidates that there was just one spot left to fill, which caused Tameka and Kai to glance nervously at each other across the room. Tameka, a talented dancer, hoped to show off her technique and style in the show, while Kai, a gifted pianist, dreamed of becoming a professional musician and wanted this opportunity to perform. Though each hoped desperately to be selected, that seemed impossible now, with only two more try-outs for one opening.

Kai moved beside Tameka. "I know you're an awesome dancer, and you know I'm great on the piano. Too bad we've got to battle each other," he whispered.

"Oh, that's kind to say, but one of us is simply going to be disappointed," Tameka answered.

Kai asked, "What music are you dancing to?" Tameka replied that she planned to dance to the hit, "Sweet, Fleet Feet." Kai originally planned to play a classical waltz by Frederic Chopin. But he also knew "Sweet, Fleet Feet" and could play it energetically, so he suggested something to Tameka that made her grin.

Then Ms. Spira turned to Tameka and Kai to ask, "Who's next?"

"Both of us—we've become a team!" they responded. The friends chattered as they went onto the stage. "May we please have a few moments to warm up?" Tameka politely asked.

Text Marking

The story describes a problem. Identify it and think about how the characters responded to it and found a way out.

☐ Box the conflict.

◯ Circle the ways that Kai and Tameka reacted to the conflict.

___ <u>Underline</u> the resolution.

Literary Passages: Close Reading (Grade 5)
© Scholastic Inc.

Name _____ Date _____

Talent Show Contest

▶ **Answer each question. Give details from the entertainment story.**

1 Who is telling the story?

○ A. Ms. Spira ○ B. Tameka ○ C. Kai ○ D. a narrator

What helped you answer? _____

_____

_____

2 Two words that could describe everyone auditioning for the talent show are...

○ A. ...dancers and pianists. ○ C. ...hopefuls and candidates.

○ B. ...best friends and hopefuls. ○ D. ...jugglers and musicians.

What helped you answer? _____

_____

_____

3 Why did Tameka ask Ms. Spira for a few moments to warm up?

_____

_____

_____

_____

_____

_____

4 What inferences can you make about Kai based on his idea?

_____

_____

_____

_____

_____

_____

_____

Name _____ Date _____

The Unlucky Lizard

Read the African-American folktale.
Then follow the directions in the Text Marking box.

Ages back, Lizard and Frog both sat upright like dogs. Then came the day that things changed forever for Lizard. The pair were strolling along a dusty trail near their swamp. Around a bend they noticed a lush green field with a clear blue pond. They hankered for a visit, but a sturdy wooden fence blocked the way.

"I'd surely love a swim in that sweet water," said Frog longingly.

"I'd surely love to catch some fine insects there," pined Lizard.

So the two approached the fence, which seemed to grow taller and more threatening with each step. To make things worse, the fence boards fit snugly together and were buried deep in the ground. They saw no possibility to clamber over nor dig under.

Frog and Lizard sat upright like dogs by that frustrating fence, pondering how to get to the other side. Then Frog spied a thin crevice near the ground. "I'm gonna squeeze myself through," he announced. So he shoved and squirmed and wriggled until he popped out on the other side!

"Your turn, Lizard," Frog hollered. So Lizard scuttled to the crack. He pressed and squashed and struggled to get through. He pushed so hard that a fence board tumbled and flattened him. After that, Lizard never again sat like a dog, but could only slither close to the ground. Frog and Lizard remained friends despite Lizards' flatter appearance.

⭐ Text Marking

Use context clues to unlock meaning.

◯ Circle the words **longingly, clamber,** and **crevice.**

▭ Box the expression **hankered for.**

___ Underline context clues for each of the words and the phrase.

Literary Passages: Close Reading (Grade 5)
© Scholastic Inc.

Name _____ Date _____

The Unlucky Lizard

▶ **Answer each question. Give details from the folktale.**

1 If you were to *clamber* over something, you would most likely be…

  ○ A. arguing.   ○ B. climbing.   ○ C. slithering.   ○ D. wondering.

What helped you answer? _____

_____

_____

2 According to this folktale, what did Frog and Lizard share a *hankering* for?

  ○ A. making new friends   ○ C. sitting upright like dogs can

  ○ B. having a refreshing swim   ○ D. getting past a fence to a field and pond

What helped you answer? _____

_____

_____

3 Describe a situation when using the word *longingly* makes sense.

_____

_____

_____

_____

_____

_____

4 What lesson do you think Lizard might have learned from this tale?

_____

_____

_____

_____

_____

_____

_____

Literary Passages: Close Reading (Grade 5)
© Scholastic Inc.

The Shipwreck

Read the fable, adapted from Aesop.
Then follow the directions in the Text Marking box.

Long ago, when dolphins were friendly toward humans, shipwrecked sailors often told of being rescued by holding onto a dolphin's back for a ride to shore. Also at that time, ships commonly carried animal mascots, like monkeys, who were known to be smart, entertaining companions, and good at mimicking the sailors.

One stormy night near Athens, Greece, a ship broke apart, dumping its sailors into the sea. Struggling, they grabbed onto anything they could to stay afloat. Emulating them, the monkey clung to an oar.

A dolphin swimming past, mistaking the monkey for a sailor, invited him to climb onto her back and grasp her tightly while she carried him to land. She politely asked, "Are you from Greece?"

"Yes, my family is from Athens," replied the monkey.

"You sound like a well-educated person," said the dolphin respectfully. So the monkey began to regale her with fantastical tales; but all were lies. Soon the dolphin interrupted the monkey's yammering to indicate land on the horizon.

"As an Athenian," the dolphin said, "you must surely know Piraeus."

"Naturally!" the monkey replied. "Piraeus is my father's first cousin, whom we visit often because he is our favorite relative."

Knowing that Piraeus was the port nearest Athens, the dolphin realized the monkey was an imposter. So she dove under the waves, letting the monkey swim on his own, and sought an honest man to save.

Text Marking

Use context clues to unlock meaning.

◯ Circle the words **mascots, emulating, regale,** and **yammering.**

_____ Underline context clues for each.

The Shipwreck

▶ **Answer each question. Give details from the fable.**

1 Which word is a synonym for *mimicking*?

○ A. realizing   ○ B. emulating   ○ C. yammering   ○ D. entertaining

What helped you answer? _____

_____

_____

2 Which is the most appropriate moral for this fable?

○ A. Look before you leap.   ○ C. A liar deceives no one but himself.

○ B. The memory of a good deed lives.   ○ D. A friend in need is a friend indeed.

What helped you answer? _____

_____

_____

3 According to this fable, why did sailors bring animals aboard ship?

_____

_____

_____

_____

_____

4 Why did the dolphin dive under the waves at the end?

_____

_____

_____

_____

_____

_____

_____

Literary Passages: Close Reading (Grade 5)
© Scholastic Inc.

Name _____ Date _____

Room and Bored

Read the family story.
Then follow the directions in the Text Marking box.

Luckily, Kenji has his own bedroom, but he had outgrown it. About to enter middle school, why would he want a room with a kiddie desk and dinosaur curtains? With that in mind, Kenji asked his parents if he could bring his room up to speed. To his delight, they agreed, and together they examined the room with an eye for how they could renovate it.

The bed was the first thing to go, replaced by a bunk bed for sleepover guests. Its comforter, decorated with cartoon animals, also had to go. "Soccer balls might be better," Kenji suggested. His mother agreed to shop for different curtains, too.

Similarly, the tiny desk had outlived its use; a new computer station would provide a welcome contrast. The water color paintings on the wall, which he'd made in third grade, also had to go, along with the pirate toy chest. Rather, he'd hang up pictures of tennis players he admired and get a bookcase.

On the other hand, Kenji was content with his room's pale green color. "That's the same color as the seats at the stadium," he explained. And the rug was okay, he thought, despite its stains.

When the upgrade was completed, the change in the character of the room was apparent. At peace in his more mature environment, Kenji felt ready for his new school.

Text Marking

Compare and contrast the before-and-after appearances of Kenji's room.

☐ Box signal words for comparing and contrasting.

◯ Circle the ways the room will stay the same.

___ Underline the ways it will be different.

Name _____ Date _____

Room and Bored

▶ **Answer each question. Give details from the family story.**

1 What does Kenji mean by asking to bring his room *up to speed*?

○ A. Hang pictures of fast athletes.   ○ C. Make it age-appropriate.

○ B. Fill it with newer furniture.   ○ D. Fix it up quickly.

What helped you answer? _____

_____

_____

2 Which is a synonym for *renovate*?

○ A. upgrade   ○ B. keep the same   ○ C. tidy up   ○ D. remove

What helped you answer? _____

_____

_____

3 Summarize the change in character of the before-and-after versions of Kenji's room.

_____

_____

_____

_____

_____

4 What theme does this story explore?

_____

_____

_____

_____

_____

_____

_____

Literary Passages: Close Reading (Grade 5)
© Scholastic Inc.

Name _____ Date _____

The Chapman Stick

Read the music story.
Then follow the directions in the Text Marking box.

At the music museum, I got to see new and ancient instruments from around the world. They were all quite fascinating! Then I learned that there was going to be a demonstration of a special instrument called a Chapman Stick.

"Good afternoon," said a musician. "Please welcome my band." I was puzzled, because he was by himself. There weren't any other band members on stage beside him. He held something that looked like a guitar, only it didn't have a body. The entire instrument consisted of just a fretboard, which was wider and longer than a guitar's fretboard. It had more strings than a guitar, too.

He plugged the Chapman Stick into an electric amplifier, just like a guitar. Then he began to play. I couldn't believe my ears. I was amazed by all the different sounds the Chapman Stick could make. The instrument sounded like a guitar, a piano, a bass, and a drum, all at the same time. I enjoyed hearing the musician play full songs all by himself.

I wish I had a Chapman Stick. I could be a one-boy band. I know what I'm requesting for my birthday this year!

Text Marking

Compare and contrast the Chapman Stick with an electric guitar.

☐ Box signal words for comparing and contrasting.

◯ Circle the ways the instruments are alike.

___ Underline the ways they are different.

Literary Passages: Close Reading (Grade 5)
© Scholastic Inc.

Name _____ Date _____

The Chapman Stick

▶ **Answer each question. Give details from the music story.**

1 Something that is *ancient* must be _____.

○ A. electronic　　○ B. very old　　○ C. musical　　○ D. unique

What helped you answer? _____

_____

_____

2 From whose point of view is this story told?

○ A. the musician　○ B. a museum guide　○ C. a museum visitor　○ D. a pianist

What helped you answer? _____

_____

_____

3 What inference can you make about the storyteller?

_____

_____

_____

_____

_____

4 Look at the illustrations. Compare and contrast the fretboards of the Chapman Stick and the electric guitar.

_____

_____

_____

_____

_____

_____

_____

Have You Ever Seen?

Read the poem.
Then follow the directions in the Text Marking box.

Have you ever seen a sheet on a river bed?

Or a single hair from a hammer's head?

Has the foot of a mountain any toes?

And is there a pair of garden hose?

Does the needle ever wink its eye?

Why doesn't the wing of a building fly?

Can you tickle the ribs of a parasol?

Or open the trunk of a tree at all?

Are the teeth of a rake ever going to bite?

Have the hands of a clock any left or right?

Can the garden plot be deep and dark?

And what is the sound of a birch's bark?

Writers use **figurative language**
to describe one thing by comparing
it with something else.

Examples: • a *carpet* of flowers
          • a *blanket* of fog

★ Text Marking ★

Make an inference: What makes
this poem amusing and interesting?

X   the literary strategy
       the poet uses throughout.

    ☐ flashback

    ☐ exaggeration

    ☐ figurative language

_____ <u>Underline</u> words or phrases
in each line that have
multiple meanings.

 Think about what you
already know.

Name _____ Date _____

Have You Ever Seen?

▶ **Answer each question. Give details from the poem.**

1 Which type of *hose* does the poet joke about in the first stanza?

○ A. stockings   ○ B. slippers   ○ C. watering can   ○ D. plastic tubing

What helped you answer? _____

_____

_____

2 Where would you be most likely to find a *deep and dark plot*?

○ A. on a hike   ○ B. on a graph   ○ C. in a garden   ○ D. in a mystery

What helped you answer? _____

_____

_____

3 In your own words, what point is the poet trying to get across?

_____

_____

_____

_____

_____

_____

4 Why does each line in this poem ask a question without ever giving an answer?

_____

_____

_____

_____

_____

_____

_____

To Go or Not to Go

Read the science fiction story.
Then follow the directions in the Text Marking box.

"It's the opportunity of a lifetime, Rashid. We'll be pioneers!" said Dr. Donovan.

Despite his mother's enthusiasm, Rashid wasn't convinced that joining a new colony on Mars was a good idea. "But Mom," he said, "we'd have to stay there at *least* two years. And when you add on the six months or more it will take to get there and the same to return, we'd be away from home and friends for three years—or longer! It'll be 2051 when we finally get back, and I'll be sixteen already!"

"But Rashid, just think of the advantages, not the least of which is how much time we'll spend together as a family."

Unconvinced, Rashid responded, "Mom, taking this trip is not only unappealing, but probably unhealthy, too. We'll be exposed to deep-space radiation. Plus, life in that planet's low-gravity environment might be too weird. For instance, what will we do for entertainment? I don't expect we'll find swimming pools, hockey rinks, or restaurants!"

Rashid's mother knew all this, but she was passionate about going, believing that after preparation and study, they could meet each potential challenge. "Just think how exciting it would be, darling," she replied, "an experience like no other. How can I encourage you to be as excited as I am about this chance for adventure?"

"I'm not that excited to bring back Martian microbes, Mom. Can I go to hockey practice now?"

★ Text Marking ★

Make an inference: How does the story reveal the personalities of Rashid and his mother?

_____ Underline text clues.

 Think about what you already know.

Literary Passages: Close Reading (Grade 5)
© Scholastic Inc.

Name _____   Date _____

To Go or Not to Go

▶ **Answer each question. Give details from the science fiction story.**

1 Something is *the opportunity of a lifetime* if it is _____.

○ A. challenging   ○ B. dangerous   ○ C. lively   ○ D. rare

What helped you answer? _____

_____

_____

2 Which description best fits Dr. Donovan?

○ A. argumentative   ○ B. cautious   ○ C. passionate   ○ D. timid

What helped you answer? _____

_____

_____

3 Based on the story, what kind of person is Rashid? In what ways is his personality different from his mother's?

_____

_____

_____

_____

_____

_____

_____

4 What details in the story indicate that it is a work of science fiction?

_____

_____

_____

_____

_____

_____

Egg of Chaos

Read the Chinese creation myth.
Then follow the directions in the Text Marking box.

At first, the universe was jumbled inside a huge egg. That murky chaos contained all forms of opposites, or *yin* and *yang*. In the whirling mixture were water and fire, night and day, north and south, and so on. And there was Pangu, the being who would one day create our world.

Pangu slept inside the egg of chaos for 18,000 years. During that time, the *yin* and *yang* of all things was tangled together. He separated the heavier *yin* from the lighter *yang*. The *yang* floated up to become the sky while the *yin* settled to become the earth.

Standing between the two parts, Pangu's head touched sky and his feet strode upon earth. Over the next 18,000 years, sky and earth grew ever more vast, moving apart by ten feet each day.

Pangu also grew, keeping sky and earth separated. By the time of his death, earth and sky had settled into their places. One of Pangu's eyes became the sun, the other the moon. His breath became wind and clouds; his voice turned into the sound of thunder. Pangu's body formed great mountains and his blood its flowing waters. His veins became roads and his muscles fertile fields. His hairs remained in the sky as glittering stars.

Text Marking

Summarize the story.

◯ Circle the main idea of the story.

_____ Underline important details.

Name _____ Date _____

Egg of Chaos

▶ **Answer each question. Give details from the creation myth.**

1 Which best describes the concept of *yin* and *yang*?

○ A. powers of creation ○ B. entanglement ○ C. opposites ○ D. chaos

What helped you answer? _____

_____

_____

2 How did earth and sky stay separated?

○ A. The egg of chaos expanded. ○ C. Earth and sky grew 10 feet each day.

○ B. Pangu grew and kept them apart. ○ D. The myth does not explain this.

What helped you answer? _____

_____

_____

3 According to Chinese belief, *yin* and *yang* are opposite forces that are also related in some way. Explain how health and sickness are examples of *yin* and *yang*.

_____

_____

_____

_____

_____

4 Summarize how the actions of Pangu influenced how the world came to be.

_____

_____

_____

_____

_____

_____

Literary Passages: Close Reading (Grade 5)
© Scholastic Inc.

Febold Feboldson's Find

Read the tall tale from the American Midwest.
Then follow the directions in the Text Marking box.

You've probably tasted the popular American popcorn ball. You might imagine some cook thinking to use syrup to stick popcorn together into a tasty snack. Well, that's NOT how popcorn balls came to be, at least according to old Febold Feboldson. He claimed that the popcorn ball invented itself during the weird summer of 1874.

Midwestern farmers called that growing season The Year of Striped Weather. That's because it alternated rainy and hot, not day by day, but by sections of cropland. Fields grew in stripes: first you'd see a mile-wide stripe of crops wilting in the broiling heat, then a mile-wide stripe of waterlogged crops soaking nearly to death.

Febold Feboldson had this situation on his farm. He grew corn in the Dismal River valley and sugar cane on the hills above. One day the sun baked his corn plants so hot that the kernels popped, causing a yellow blizzard.

Text Marking

Summarize the story.
Think about its theme.

◯   Circle the main idea of the story.

_____   <u>Underline</u> important details.

Meanwhile, the rain was drenching his sugar cane stalks so badly that the syrup inside washed out and rolled toward the popcorn. A ball soon formed, growing gigantic as it tumbled along. Febold estimated the giant popcorn ball at about two hundred feet wide!

His neighbor, Bert Bergstrom, witnessed this eye-popping event. Bert offered to help Febold corral the great popcorn ball to impress visitors. But just then, a swarm of hungry grasshoppers devoured the entire very-first popcorn ball.

Febold Feboldson's Find

▶ **Answer each question. Give details from the tall tale.**

1   What odd thing happened during The Year of Striped Weather?

    ○ A. Strange weather made crops grow in striped sections.

    ○ B. Farmers planted their crops only at night.

    ○ C. The only crops that grew had stripes on them.

    ○ D. Febold Feboldson met Bert Bergstrom.

    What helped you answer? _____

_____

_____

2   Which word does NOT mean the same as the other three?

    ○ A. soaked   ○ B. drenched   ○ C. tumbled   ○ D. waterlogged

    What helped you answer? _____

_____

_____

3   Explain the meaning of the title of this passage.

_____

_____

_____

_____

4   Why do you think the tall tale ends with grasshoppers devouring the entire popcorn ball?

_____

_____

_____

_____

_____

_____

_____

Literary Passages: Close Reading (Grade 5)
© Scholastic Inc.

Answer Key

Fishing With Grandpa Leon

Read the realistic fiction.
Then follow the directions in the Text Marking box.

(Ronan) was beside himself with excitement. He was ten years old and his (Grandpa Leon) was finally going to take him fishing. Grandpa Leon claimed to be "a fishing expert, practically a professional angler." He told Ronan that he'd caught giant marlin and huge tuna, and that he had many adventurous stories to tell. He promised he'd supply all the fishing gear: rods, reels, hooks, bait, buckets, and plenty of food, too. All Ronan had to do was to be ready promptly at 6 AM.

As it happened, it was good Grandpa Leon brought plenty of food because grandfather and grandson had plenty of time to eat it. The fish simply weren't biting. "They're napping," he informed Ronan, knowingly.

No nibbles left plenty of time for Grandpa Leon's elaborate fish stories. In fact, it was during one of those tall tales that Ronan suddenly felt a sharp tug on his line. "I've got something really huge!" he shouted.

"Hold tight, I'll help," Grandpa Leon replied, reaching over and grabbing the rod. Together, they tugged on the line that held what promised to be a colossal, prize-winning fish. Finally, they reeled in their catch—a tattered leather suitcase, heavy with sand.

"How about that, Ronan—the first suitcase of the day!" Grandpa Leon exclaimed, adding, "You can't say it wasn't a big catch!"

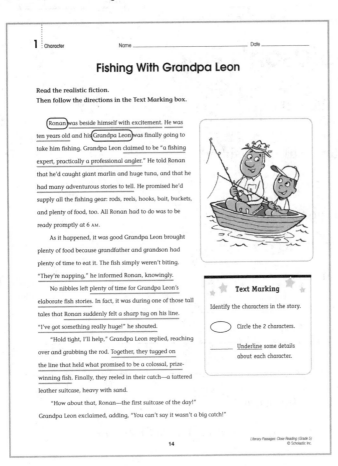

Text Marking

Identify the characters in the story.

⬭ Circle the 2 characters.

___ Underline some details about each character.

14

Literary Passages: Close Reading (Grade 5)
© Scholastic Inc.

A Cabin in Syracuse, 1855

Read the historical fiction.
Then follow the directions in the Text Marking box.

In the years before the Civil War, some concerned citizens teamed up to assist runaway slaves in their perilous effort to escape bondage. They formed a network of safe houses along the routes north. (Elijah)'s cabin in Syracuse, New York, was part of this Underground Railroad.

One blustery winter night, the family awoke to frantic rapping at the door. Elijah opened it to see [Amos,] a friend from nearby Manlius, with two runaways—a young woman and a small girl, both looking terrified and both shivering in drenched, tattered clothes.

"Come, sit by our fire," said [Elijah's mother,] who was welcoming. "I'll have Elijah get it roaring again, and then I'll find you some dry clothes and warm food."

"Oh, thank you kindly, ma'am," replied the woman as the two runaways entered. "I'm [Nola,] and we've been running hard for days. My little [Ruby] here is powerful hungry."

Meanwhile, Elijah listened carefully to his instructions from Amos. "You'll keep them here two days," he said gravely. "Best get your hiding space ready, as slave catchers have been spotted nearby."

Flashing two fingers to signal his mother, Elijah then sat with the guests as they ate and drank heartily. *How long had it been since their last meal,* he wondered. [Whiskers] trotted over to meet the strangers. Ruby timidly stroked the furry cat and smiled—possibly for the first time in days.

Text Marking

Identify who the story is about.

⬭ Circle the main character.

☐ Box the other characters.

___ Underline details about each character.

16

Literary Passages: Close Reading (Grade 5)
© Scholastic Inc.

◀ Sample Text Markings

Passage 1: Fishing With Grandpa Leon

1. D; Sample answer: I picked D because it's the only answer that makes sense, and I found a context clue in the first paragraph.

2. A; Sample answer: I picked A because Grandpa Leon seems upbeat and hopeful about the fishing trip.

3. Sample answer: I think Ronan would say that the trip had many long boring stretches because the fish weren't biting, but he was entertained by Grandpa Leon's stories and did enjoy making the first "catch."

4. Sample answer: He acted as if the suitcase itself was a prized catch, and didn't seem the least bit disappointed.

◀ Sample Text Markings

Passage 2: A Cabin in Syracuse, 1855

1. D; Sample answer: I picked D because I could tell that the story was told in the third person.

2. B; Sample answer: I picked B because I understood in paragraph 1 that slavery was what the runaways were trying to escape.

3. Sample answer: I think Elijah is against slavery and is brave enough to offer help to the desperate runaway slaves. He is caring, determined, and helpful.

4. Sample answer: The opening paragraph provides some historical background about the time and place where the story is set.

The Expedition

Read the adventure story.
Then follow the directions in the Text Marking box.

They'd been trapped by ice for 36 days and had been on their own for longer than that, ever since a storm separated them from the ship and the rest of the crew on their expedition. Karl was in a pitiful state—lost, weak, frightened, and shivering from unrelenting cold. He was also suffering the painful effects of frostbite.

Suddenly, ice cracked enough for the boat to break loose and begin to bob gently in the frigid sea. The crew cheered their good fortune. No longer stuck in the ice, their chances of survival had edged up a notch. But Karl understood that the struggles had not ended, as medical supplies were nearly gone and there was barely any food left. If that weren't terrifying enough, the maps were lost, too.

The crew navigated icy waters until their hands bled and muscles ached. For days, Karl saw nothing in the muted, constant light but other ice floes. Then, finally, he detected a sound in the stillness that he hadn't heard for months: the cawing of birds. That sweet sound signaled that land was near. All were exhilarated!

The land they found was snow-covered and flat. The crew rowed along its barren coast until they spotted the mouth of a river. Karl and the men entered, presuming it would lead to a village and safety. On they plodded, ever more hopeful of survival.

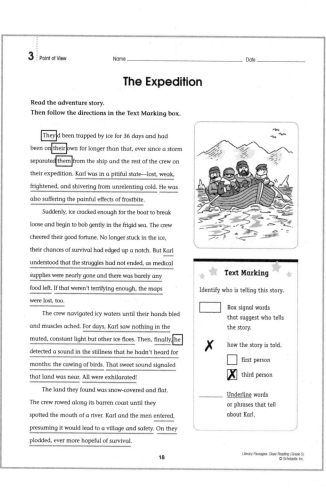

★ **Text Marking** ★

Identify who is telling this story.

☐ Box signal words that suggest who tells the story.

✗ how the story is told.

☐ first person

☒ third person

___ Underline words or phrases that tell about Karl.

18

Literary Passages: Close Reading (Grade 5)
© Scholastic Inc.

Passage 3: The Expedition

1. C; Sample answer: I picked C because although the story includes boats, nature, and weather, the main issue in the story is whether, when, and how the crew will survive their terrible and challenging ordeal.

2. A; Sample answer: I picked A because I understood that the crew had been in a very cold situation for a long time, and *constant* is the best synonym.

3. Sample answer: The narrator knew that although circumstances had improved, survival was still uncertain.

4. Sample answer: I think the story takes place in a very cold climate, perhaps in the Arctic Sea, because there is ice, frozen for long stretches, barren lands, and near-constant light.

The Record Setter

Read the humorous story.
Then follow the directions in the Text Marking box.

My brother, Alex, is generally considered to be a reliable, clever, thoughtful fellow. I say "generally" because of things like what he's doing right now.

Picture this and you'll understand. While I, Nate, sit here playing a video game and texting with half my friends—two perfectly normal things to be doing for amusement—what is he occupied with? Alex is standing over there, counting softly to himself 79, 80, 81, 82… while he repeatedly bats a rubber ball attached by an elastic string to a wooden paddle. This is nonsensical behavior, is it not?

You might think I'm being too hard on Alex, as brothers sometimes can be to one another. On the contrary, I'm being lenient. You see, this time it's paddle-ball batting, but the last time—and I refer to just a few weeks ago—the challenge was standing on his head for as long as he could, with a timer set up on the rug. Of course, he had to read it upside down, but I suppose he got better at it day by day. Maybe he should've put the timer upside down, too.

Frankly, I'm getting a bit concerned. What if one of his goofy pals introduces him to alligator wrestling? Or what if he gets enticed to take up tightrope walking from skyscraper to skyscraper? I tell you, for Alex, these ideas are not too far-fetched!

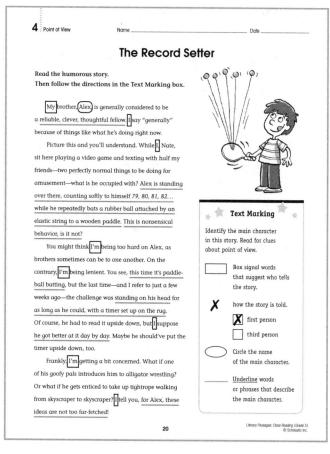

★ **Text Marking** ★

Identify the main character in this story. Read for clues about point of view.

☐ Box signal words that suggest who tells the story.

✗ how the story is told.

☒ first person

☐ third person

◯ Circle the name of the main character.

___ Underline words or phrases that describe the main character.

20

Literary Passages: Close Reading (Grade 5)
© Scholastic Inc.

Passage 4: The Record Setter

1. D; Sample answer: I picked D because Nate says in the second paragraph that he likes playing video games and considers that normal behavior.

2. A; Sample answer: I picked A because *easygoing* seems to be the opposite of being too hard on Alex.

3. Sample answer: Although Alex may do things that Nate finds peculiar, Alex probably has no intention of taking up alligator wrestling or tightrope walking.

4. Sample answer: Alex might poke fun at Nate for all the time he wastes on video games and texting with his friends.

The Beach House

Read the suspense story.
Then follow the directions in the Text Marking box.

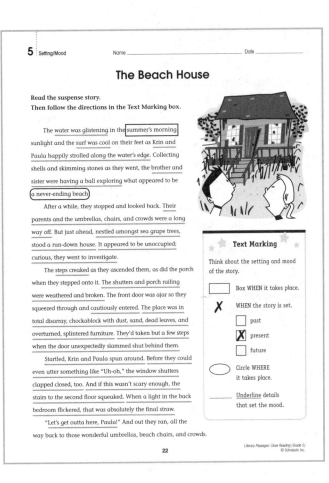

The water was glistening in the summer's morning sunlight and the surf was cool on their feet as Krin and Paula happily strolled along the water's edge. Collecting shells and skimming stones as they went, the brother and sister were having a ball exploring what appeared to be a never-ending beach.

After a while, they stopped and looked back. Their parents and the umbrellas, chairs, and crowds were a long way off. But just ahead, nestled amongst sea grape trees, stood a run-down house. It appeared to be unoccupied; curious, they went to investigate.

The steps creaked as they ascended them, as did the porch when they stepped onto it. The shutters and porch railing were weathered and broken. The front door was ajar so they squeezed through and cautiously entered. The place was in total disarray, chockablock with dust, sand, dead leaves, and overturned, splintered furniture. They'd taken but a few steps when the door unexpectedly slammed shut behind them.

Startled, Krin and Paula spun around. Before they could even utter something like "Uh-oh," the window shutters clapped closed, too. And if this wasn't scary enough, the stairs to the second floor squeaked. When a light in the back bedroom flickered, that was absolutely the final straw.

"Let's get outta here, Paula!" And out they ran, all the way back to those wonderful umbrellas, beach chairs, and crowds.

Text Marking

Think about the setting and mood of the story.

☐ Box WHEN it takes place.

✗ WHEN the story is set.
  ☐ past
  ☒ present
  ☐ future

◯ Circle WHERE it takes place.

___ Underline details that set the mood.

22

Literary Passages: Close Reading (Grade 5)
© Scholastic Inc.

◀ Sample Text Markings ·

Passage 5: The Beach House

1. C; Sample answer: I picked C because I could tell that it is written in third person (*he, they*), and it probably wasn't told by a ghost.

2. B; Sample answer: I picked B because according to the description, the inside of the house is crowded with lots of stuff.

3. Sample answer: I think the haunted house scared them a lot, which made them grateful to be safely back among their parents and the crowds on the beach.

4. Sample answer: The story is set on a long beach on a summer morning. At first, the mood is pleasant as the two happy strollers are enjoying a lovely, relaxing day. The mood turns more creepy and scary when the pair enters a vacant house that unexpectedly seems haunted.

Mile-and-a-Quarter Monkey

Read the descriptive story.
Then follow the directions in the Text Marking box.

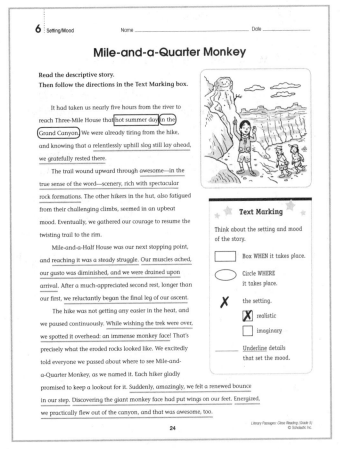

It had taken us nearly five hours from the river to reach Three-Mile House that hot summer day in the Grand Canyon. We were already tiring from the hike, and knowing that a relentlessly uphill slog still lay ahead, we gratefully rested there.

The trail wound upward through awesome—in the true sense of the word—scenery, rich with spectacular rock formations. The other hikers in the hut, also fatigued from their challenging climbs, seemed in an upbeat mood. Eventually, we gathered our courage to resume the twisting trail to the rim.

Mile-and-a-Half House was our next stopping point, and reaching it was a steady struggle. Our muscles ached, our gusto was diminished, and we were drained upon arrival. After a much-appreciated second rest, longer than our first, we reluctantly began the final leg of our ascent.

The hike was not getting any easier in the heat, and we paused continuously. While wishing the trek were over, we spotted it overhead: an immense monkey face! That's precisely what the eroded rocks looked like. We excitedly told everyone we passed about where to see Mile-and-a-Quarter Monkey, as we named it. Each hiker gladly promised to keep a lookout for it. Suddenly, amazingly, we felt a renewed bounce in our step. Discovering the giant monkey face had put wings on our feet. Energized, we practically flew out of the canyon, and that was awesome, too.

Text Marking

Think about the setting and mood of the story.

☐ Box WHEN it takes place.

◯ Circle WHERE it takes place.

✗ the setting.
  ☒ realistic
  ☐ imaginary

___ Underline details that set the mood.

24

Literary Passages: Close Reading (Grade 5)
© Scholastic Inc.

◀ Sample Text Markings

Passage 6: Mile-and-a-Quarter Monkey

1. C; Sample answer: I picked C since the hikers were in a grumpy mood because they were so hot and tired, even though they were having a great hike.

2. B; Sample answer: I picked B because I gathered from the story that the hike, also called a trek, was strenuous and exhausting, much like a lengthy hike in snow.

3. Sample answer: The hikers walked in the hot summer heat on a trail that was steep, winding, and uphill.

4. Sample answer: Noticing a rock formation that looked like a giant monkey was a funny discovery, which lifted the spirits of the hikers and gave them an energy boost.

Medieval Festival

Read the fantasy.
Then follow the directions in the Text Marking box.

Driving to the Medieval Festival, Mom sang old folksongs while Gavin studied the long list of events. There would be sword classes, blacksmithing, acrobats, dancers, jesters, and more, but it was jousting that was his top priority.

When the two entered the festival grounds, a whirl of sights, sounds, and smells overwhelmed them. Sheep and goats grazed beside horses and mules. The scent of fresh cider perfumed the air while strolling jugglers and musicians entertained the crowds. As Gavin pulled Mom toward the jousting field, he was so busy gawking that he tripped and fell. When he arose, his mother was gone and his body felt unusually heavy. Yikes! He was wearing a full suit of armor!

"Sir, your steed awaits!" announced a man in a cloak, directing Gavin toward the stable. Too stunned to protest, Gavin clanked along, huffing under the armor's weight.

"I think you're mistaken," Gavin sputtered.

"Not so!" replied the squire. "Queen Mab commands you to replace Sir Harry, who broke his arm yesterday. Ride proudly to honor her!"

Gavin gulped, feeling equally confused and thrilled at this crazy turn of events. He'd wanted to see a joust, but to actually participate in one? Zounds!

The squire paraded Gavin and his horse into position and handed him the long pole. Across the field was his fierce opponent, fully armored and ready...

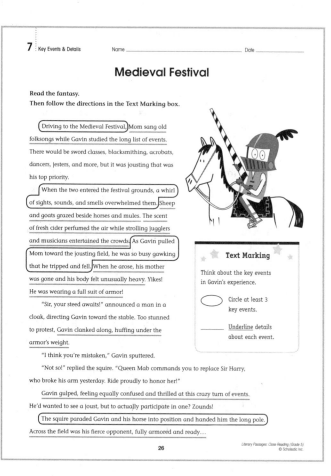

Text Marking

Think about the key events in Gavin's experience.

⬭ Circle at least 3 key events.

___ Underline details about each event.

26

Literary Passages: Close Reading (Grade 5)
© Scholastic Inc.

Passage 7: Medieval Festival

1. C; Sample answer: I picked C because this is the most logical choice.

2. A; Sample answer: I picked A because I pictured Gavin trying to take in all the sights and not paying attention, which is probably why he tripped.

3. Sample answer: The story starts out in the present, with Gavin and his mom attending a Medieval Festival. But his fall seems to cause him to travel back into medieval times, where he isn't a kid but is suddenly a knight jousting for his queen.

4. Sample answer: Although Gavin was interested in seeing a joust performed, it's a completely different experience to actually participate in such a dangerous and fierce physical competition.

Block Party Celebrity

Read the community story.
Then follow the directions in the Text Marking box.

Newly moved in and eager to meet their neighbors, the Guerrero family had a great idea. They would serve Rosa's delicious *elote*, a favorite savory dip made with corn and cheese, at the block party.

They set up their table in front of their house, located at the quiet end of the block, far from the busy avenue. The family was in a jovial mood as they set up aluminum trays of *elote*, tortilla chips, plastic bowls, forks, and napkins.

Despite the appealing aroma of corn, few people strolled over, distracted by temptations elsewhere on the block. With few neighbors to serve, Ms. Guerrero permitted Yimi and Luisa to explore. When they returned, ice creams in hand, a commotion grabbed their attention. It was the town's mayor, Elena Carillo-Lopez, and her entourage. They had arrived at the Guerrero's end of the block.

The mayor stopped first at their table, smiling warmly as Luisa heaped *elote* into a bowl, added some chips, a fork, and served it with a napkin. "Holy *guacamole*, your *elote* is the best!" the mayor exclaimed, glowing with each mouthful.

Rosa blushed, saying, "*Gracias, señora.*"

Well, that did it. It seemed now that everybody else made a bee-line to the Guerrero table for *elote*. They were newcomers no longer.

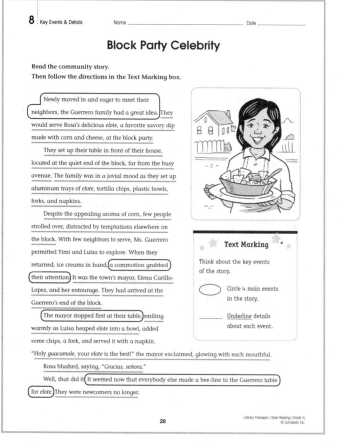

Text Marking

Think about the key events of the story.

⬭ Circle 4 main events in the story.

___ Underline details about each event.

28

Literary Passages: Close Reading (Grade 5)
© Scholastic Inc.

Passage 8: Block Party Celebrity

1. D; Sample answer: I picked D because it says that the Guerreros are new to the neighborhood and eager to meet their neighbors.

2. B; Sample answer: I picked B because it says that in the last paragraph.

3. Sample answer: Their corn dish helped introduce them to their neighbors and to feel like part of their new community.

4. Sample answer: Although the mayor seems to be the celebrity, the true celebrity is actually Rosa Guerrero because of the quality of her elote.

9 Sequence of Events Name _____ Date _____

Painted Sneakers

Read the crafts story.
Then follow the directions in the Text Marking box.

(1) Packing my van by 7 AM gives me time to get to the lake for this autumn's crafts market. The winding drive will be lovely, as will the reunions with my fellow craftspeople, folks I see once a year.

(2) Before coffee and chit-chat, I set up my booth. First I assemble the lightweight aluminum poles that frame my protective canopy. After all, the market takes place come rain or shine. Then I set up my tables and racks to hold my one-of-a-kind, hand-painted sneakers. I put my most popular superhero and cartoon pairs on racks so their designs attract customers. Next I set out other items—wild laces, goofy flip-flops, hair ornaments—neatly in trays.

(3) After that, I set out an album showing all my designs for customers to flip through, and a sign-up book for people who want to get on my mailing list.

(4) Customers start arriving by 11 AM, so everything must be ready. My last task is to activate and test my wi-fi payment machine so I can accept cash and credit cards. At that point, my sneakers and I are prepared for the market to open.

  I stand most of the day—wearing my favorite sneakers—but rarely feel tired. Most shoppers are friendly and curious, which encourages me to tell more about my work. Occasionally, I slip away for a quick snack. Once in a while, I even sit

(5) down…! At 6 PM, when the market closes, I pack, load my van, and return home.

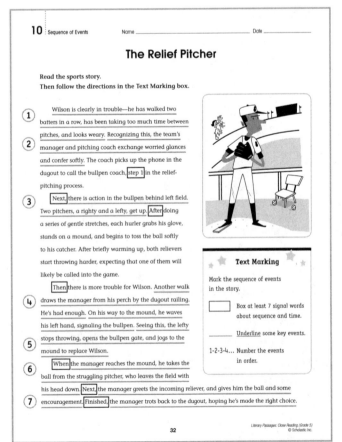

Text Marking

Mark the sequence of events in the story.

☐ Box at least 7 signal words about sequence and time.

___ Underline some key events in the painter's day.

1-2-3-4-5 Number the events in order.

30

Literary Passages: Close Reading (Grade 5)
© Scholastic Inc.

Passage 9: Painted Sneakers

1. C; Sample answer: I picked C because I could tell that the story is told in first-person because of the use of *I*, *me*, and *my*.

2. B; Sample answer: I picked B because I know this expression. It's like "the show must go on." The event will happen no matter what.

3. Sample answer: Both involve transporting the painted sneakers and other gear to or from the market. Both ends of the day require the painter to pack or unpack the goods, set up or take down the booth, and pack or unpack the van for travel.

4. Sample answer: The sneaker painter leaves home by 7 AM in order to get ready for the customers who will show up 4 hours later. The market ends by 6, so I'm guessing it will take a similar amount of time to pack up as it did to set up, plus driving time. So the painter will probably get home around 10 PM.

---

10 Sequence of Events Name _____ Date _____

The Relief Pitcher

Read the sports story.
Then follow the directions in the Text Marking box.

(1) Wilson is clearly in trouble—he has walked two batters in a row, has been taking too much time between

(2) pitches, and looks weary. Recognizing this, the team's manager and pitching coach exchange worried glances and confer softly. The coach picks up the phone in the dugout to call the bullpen coach, step 1 in the relief-pitching process.

(3) Next, there is action in the bullpen behind left field. Two pitchers, a righty and a lefty, get up. After doing a series of gentle stretches, each hurler grabs his glove, stands on a mound, and begins to toss the ball softly to his catcher. After briefly warming up, both relievers start throwing harder, expecting that one of them will likely be called into the game.

(4) Then there is more trouble for Wilson. Another walk draws the manager from his perch by the dugout railing. He's had enough. On his way to the mound, he waves his left hand, signaling the bullpen. Seeing this, the lefty

(5) stops throwing, opens the bullpen gate, and jogs to the mound to replace Wilson.

(6) When the manager reaches the mound, he takes the ball from the struggling pitcher, who leaves the field with his head down. Next, the manager greets the incoming reliever, and gives him the ball and some

(7) encouragement. Finished, the manager trots back to the dugout, hoping he's made the right choice.

Text Marking

Mark the sequence of events in the story.

☐ Box at least 7 signal words about sequence and time.

___ Underline some key events in the painter's day.

1-2-3-4… Number the events in order.

32

Literary Passages: Close Reading (Grade 5)
© Scholastic Inc.

Passage 10: The Relief Pitcher

1. A; Sample answer: I picked A because it said in paragraph 1 that calling the bullpen was Step 1 in the relief pitching process.

2. D; Sample answer: I picked D because that is the concern expressed at the beginning of the piece.

3. Sample answer: I think that the narrator knows the game of baseball very well, understands what's behind the manager's decision making, and is in a position to see everything that goes on, including what's occurring in the dugout and bullpen.

4. Sample answer: Seeing his pitcher getting tired, the team manager sets in motion a series of steps that will result in a fresh relief pitcher replacing the tired one.

Krishna's Lesson

Read the legend from India.
Then follow the directions in the Text Marking box.

Though small and gentle, young Krishna had great wisdom bestowed upon him by Lord Vishnu. In those days, Krishna lived in Vrindavan. Each year, the people there made offerings to Indra, the fierce ruler of clouds and rain, hoping to soothe Indra's temper. Krishna clearly recognized that Indra was neither generous nor sincere; he was selfish and arrogant, unworthy of respect.

To teach Indra a lesson, Krishna addressed the people. "Indra is a bully we need not serve. Instead, it makes more sense to worship Govardhan, our mountain that supports us. Let us honor kind Govardhan, who selflessly shares her lush forests and urges the clouds to shower us." The people approved Krishna's solution.

Indra flew into a mighty rage. "These farmers ignore *me* to worship a mountain on the advice of a child? I shall severely punish this insult," he thundered. Indra ordered the clouds to send furious winds and driving rains to Vrindavan. The tempest terrified the people, who fearfully sought help from young Krishna.

With supreme calm, grace, and power, Krishna lifted Govardhan into the air using only the little finger of his left hand. He steadfastly held the mountain like an umbrella, protecting Vrindavan for seven stormy days and nights.

Finally, Indra acknowledged his error. He halted the storm and deeply apologized to Krishna. Thus did humans learn not to give in to disaster.

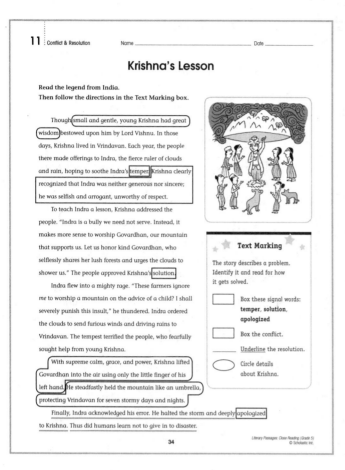

★ Text Marking ★

The story describes a problem. Identify it and read for how it gets solved.

☐ Box these signal words: **temper, solution, apologized**

☐ Box the conflict.

___ Underline the resolution.

◯ Circle details about Krishna.

34

Literary Passages: Close Reading (Grade 5)
© Scholastic Inc.

Passage 11: Krishna's Lesson

1. C; Sample answer: I picked C because Indra's actions frighten the people, who fear his temper.

2. D; Sample answer: I picked D because the details of the story made it clear that Vrindavan was a place where people lived, not a person or god.

3. Sample answer: The people feared Indra and hoped that their offerings would keep his temper under control. But when Krishna proposed a new plan, they were willing to try his solution.

4. Sample answer: Krishna was gentle, possessed wisdom from Lord Vishnu, cared about the people of Vrindavan, justified the changes he suggested, and steadfastly protected the people during the storm until Indra gave in and apologized.

Talent Show Contest

Read the entertainment story.
Then follow the directions in the Text Marking box.

Ms. Spira, the music teacher, was nearly finished auditioning hopefuls for the upcoming talent show. She announced to the two remaining candidates that there was just one spot left to fill, which caused Tameka and Kai to glance nervously at each other across the room. Tameka, a talented dancer, hoped to show off her technique and style in the show, while Kai, a gifted pianist, dreamed of becoming a professional musician and wanted this opportunity to perform. Though each hoped desperately to be selected, that seemed impossible now, with only two more try-outs for one opening.

Kai moved beside Tameka. "I know you're an awesome dancer, and you know I'm great on the piano. Too bad we've got to battle each other," he whispered.

"Oh, that's kind to say, but one of us is simply going to be disappointed," Tameka answered.

Kai asked, "What music are you dancing to?" Tameka replied that she planned to dance to the hit, "Sweet, Fleet Feet." Kai originally planned to play a classical waltz by Frederic Chopin. But he also knew "Sweet, Fleet Feet" and could play it energetically, so he suggested something to Tameka that made her grin.

Then Ms. Spira turned to Tameka and Kai to ask, "Who's next?"

"Both of us—we've become a team!" they responded. The friends chattered as they went onto the stage. "May we please have a few moments to warm up?" Tameka politely asked.

★ Text Marking ★

The story describes a problem. Identify it and think about how the characters responded to it and found a way out.

☐ Box the conflict.

◯ Circle the ways that Kai and Tameka reacted to the conflict.

___ Underline the resolution.

36

Literary Passages: Close Reading (Grade 5)
© Scholastic Inc.

Passage 12: Talent Show Contest

1. D; Sample answer: I picked D because I could tell the piece was written in third-person, so it was told by a narrator.

2. C; Sample answer: I read both of those words in the first paragraph, and understood that both described kids hoping to be chosen for the talent show.

3. Sample answer: I think Tameka was hoping for a little extra time to practice with Kai before the try-out.

4. Sample answer: Kai must feel confident enough about his musical skills to switch to a different piece at the last minute. He also must have believed that teaming up with a talented dancer would increase their chances at the talent show.

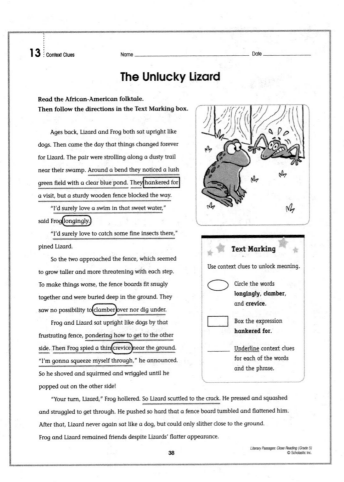

The Unlucky Lizard

Read the African-American folktale.
Then follow the directions in the Text Marking box.

Ages back, Lizard and Frog both sat upright like dogs. Then came the day that things changed forever for Lizard. The pair were strolling along a dusty trail near their swamp. Around a bend they noticed a lush green field with a clear blue pond. They hankered for a visit, but a sturdy wooden fence blocked the way.

"I'd surely love a swim in that sweet water," said Frog longingly.

"I'd surely love to catch some fine insects there," pined Lizard.

So the two approached the fence, which seemed to grow taller and more threatening with each step. To make things worse, the fence boards fit snugly together and were buried deep in the ground. They saw no possibility to clamber over nor dig under.

Frog and Lizard sat upright like dogs by that frustrating fence, pondering how to get to the other side. Then Frog spied a thin crevice near the ground. "I'm gonna squeeze myself through," he announced. So he shoved and squirmed and wriggled until he popped out on the other side!

"Your turn, Lizard," Frog hollered. So Lizard scuttled to the crack. He pressed and squashed and struggled to get through. He pushed so hard that a fence board tumbled and flattened him. After that, Lizard never again sat like a dog, but could only slither close to the ground. Frog and Lizard remained friends despite Lizards' flatter appearance.

Text Marking

Use context clues to unlock meaning.

◯ Circle the words **longingly, clamber,** and **crevice.**

▭ Box the expression **hankered for.**

___ Underline context clues for each of the words and the phrase.

38

Literary Passages: Close Reading (Grade 5)
© Scholastic Inc.

Passage 13: The Unlucky Lizard

1. B; Sample answer: I picked B because I figured out from the sentence that "dig under" was the opposite, so "clambering" must mean climbing over.

2. D; Sample answer: I picked D because the main idea of the story is their desire to get beyond that fence to the lush green field and clear blue pond.

3. Sample answer: I would use the word *longingly* to describe how I might want something badly while knowing it might be hard to come by. I might ask *longingly* to visit a faraway place.

4. Sample answer: He might have learned not to try to go where he wasn't wanted, or not to let a friend dare him to do something dangerous.

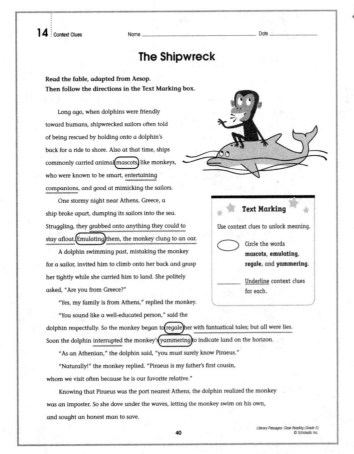

The Shipwreck

Read the fable, adapted from Aesop.
Then follow the directions in the Text Marking box.

Long ago, when dolphins were friendly toward humans, shipwrecked sailors often told of being rescued by holding onto a dolphin's back for a ride to shore. Also at that time, ships commonly carried animal mascots like monkeys, who were known to be smart, entertaining companions, and good at mimicking the sailors.

One stormy night near Athens, Greece, a ship broke apart, dumping its sailors into the sea. Struggling, they grabbed onto anything they could to stay afloat. Emulating them, the monkey clung to an oar.

A dolphin swimming past, mistaking the monkey for a sailor, invited him to climb onto her back and grasp her tightly while she carried him to land. She politely asked, "Are you from Greece?"

"Yes, my family is from Athens," replied the monkey.

"You sound like a well-educated person," said the dolphin respectfully. So the monkey began to regale her with fantastical tales; but all were lies. Soon the dolphin interrupted the monkey's yammering to indicate land on the horizon.

"As an Athenian," the dolphin said, "you must surely know Piraeus."

"Naturally!" the monkey replied. "Piraeus is my father's first cousin, whom we visit often because he is our favorite relative."

Knowing that Piraeus was the port nearest Athens, the dolphin realized the monkey was an imposter. So she dove under the waves, letting the monkey swim on his own, and sought an honest man to save.

Text Marking

Use context clues to unlock meaning.

◯ Circle the words **mascots, emulating, regale,** and **yammering.**

___ Underline context clues for each.

40

Literary Passages: Close Reading (Grade 5)
© Scholastic Inc.

Passage 14: The Shipwreck

1. B; Sample answer: I picked B because I found the word *emulating* farther down in the fable and I think it means the same.

2. C; Sample answer: I picked C because the monkey was a liar whose lies lost him the help of the dolphin.

3. Sample answer: The fable explains that the sailors enjoyed having some sort of mascot because it provided entertainment for them.

4. Sample answer: She did this to get the monkey off her back after realizing that he was a liar. She preferred to save an honest person.

Literary Passages: Close Reading (Grade 5)
© Scholastic Inc.

Name _____ Date _____

Room and Bored

Read the family story.
Then follow the directions in the Text Marking box.

Luckily, Kenji has his own bedroom, but he had outgrown it. About to enter middle school, why would he want a room with a kiddie desk and dinosaur curtains? With that in mind, Kenji asked his parents if he could bring his room up to speed. To his delight, they agreed, and together they examined the room with an eye for how they could renovate it.

The bed was the first thing to go, replaced by a bunk bed for sleepover guests. Its comforter, decorated with cartoon animals, also had to go. "Soccer balls might be better," Kenji suggested. His mother agreed to shop for different curtains, too.

Similarly, the tiny desk had outlived its use; a new computer station would provide a welcome contrast. The water color paintings on the wall, which he'd made in third grade, also had to go, along with the pirate toy chest. Rather, he'd hang up pictures of tennis players he admired and get a bookcase.

On the other hand, Kenji was content with his room's pale green color. "That's the same color as the seats at the stadium," he explained. And the rug was okay, he thought, despite its stains.

When the upgrade was completed, the change in the character of the room was apparent. At peace in his more mature environment, Kenji felt ready for his new school.

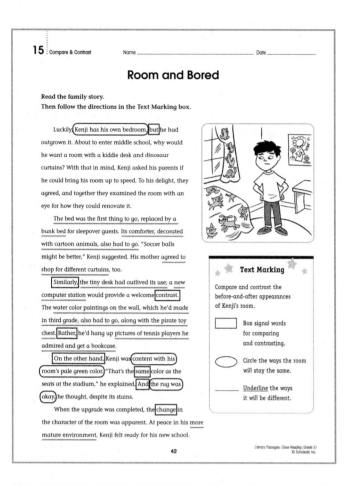

Text Marking

Compare and contrast the before-and-after appearances of Kenji's room.

☐ Box signal words for comparing and contrasting.

◯ Circle the ways the room will stay the same.

___ Underline the ways it will be different.

Literary Passages: Close Reading (Grade 5)
© Scholastic Inc.

Passage 15: Room and Bored

1. C; Sample answer: I picked C because the main idea of the story is to update Kenji's room since he's now older and more mature.

2. A; Sample answer: I picked A because I noticed the word *upgrade* in the final paragraph of the story, and it made sense.

3. Sample answer: It was babyish before the renovation. With the addition of the new furniture and décor, his room is now better suited for an older boy.

4. Sample answer: I think it explores the theme of growing up. Kenji felt out of place in his babyish room now that he was older, so he asked his parents to help it grow with him.

Name _____ Date _____

The Chapman Stick

Read the music story.
Then follow the directions in the Text Marking box.

At the music museum, I got to see new and ancient instruments from around the world. They were all quite fascinating! Then I learned that there was going to be a demonstration of a special instrument called a Chapman Stick.

"Good afternoon," said a musician. "Please welcome my band." I was puzzled, because he was by himself. There weren't any other band members on stage beside him. He held something that looked like a guitar, only it didn't have a body. The entire instrument consisted of just a fretboard, which was wider and longer than a guitar's fretboard. It had more strings than a guitar, too.

He plugged the Chapman Stick into an electric amplifier, just like a guitar. Then he began to play. I couldn't believe my ears. I was amazed by all the different sounds the Chapman Stick could make. The instrument sounded like a guitar, a piano, a bass, and a drum, all at the same time. I enjoyed hearing the musician play full songs all by himself.

I wish I had a Chapman Stick. I could be a one-boy band. I know what I'm requesting for my birthday this year!

Text Marking

Compare and contrast the Chapman Stick with an electric guitar.

☐ Box signal words for comparing and contrasting.

◯ Circle the ways the instruments are alike.

___ Underline the ways they are different.

Literary Passages: Close Reading (Grade 5)
© Scholastic Inc.

Passage 16: The Chapman Stick

1. B; Sample answer: I picked B because the museum had new and ancient instruments so I think *ancient* means very old.

2. C; Sample answer: I picked C because the story is told in first person by someone who is visiting a music museum.

3. Sample answer: I think he probably likes music because he is at a music museum, and he seems to know enough about music to appreciate learning about a new instrument.

4. Sample answer: Both fretboards are the background for the strings of the instrument. Both have tuning pegs at the top and both are long. But the Chapman Stick's fretboard is longer, wider, and supports more strings.

Literary Passages: Close Reading (Grade 5)
© Scholastic Inc.

17 Make Inferences   Name _____ Date _____

Have You Ever Seen?

Read the poem.
Then follow the directions in the Text Marking box.

Have you ever seen a sheet on a river bed?
Or a single hair from a hammer's head?
Has the foot of a mountain any toes?
And is there a pair of garden hose?

Does the needle ever wink its eye?
Why doesn't the wing of a building fly?
Can you tickle the ribs of a parasol?
Or open the trunk of a tree at all?

Are the teeth of a rake ever going to bite?
Have the hands of a clock any left or right?
Can the garden plot be deep and dark?
And what is the sound of a birch's bark?

> Writers use **figurative language**
> to describe one thing by comparing
> it with something else.
>
> *Examples:* • a carpet of flowers
>   • a blanket of fog

Text Marking

Make an inference: What makes this poem amusing and interesting?

✗ the literary strategy the poet uses throughout.

☐ flashback

☐ exaggeration

☒ figurative language

_____ Underline words or phrases in each line that have multiple meanings.

💡 Think about what you already know.

46

Literary Passages: Close Reading (Grade 5)
© Scholastic Inc.

Passage 17: Have You Ever Seen?

1. A; Sample answer: I picked A because I think *hose* is not the tube that water comes out of but the hose that comes in pairs, like stockings or panty hose.

2. D; Sample answer: I figured out that in this case, the poet was not referring to *plot* as part of a garden, but the sneaky plan of a complicated story or film.

3. Sample answer: I think the poet is pointing out words in English that have different meanings. The poet does this by asking questions that are impossible to answer if you think of the wrong meaning of a word.

4. Sample answer: Each line asks a question that makes you think about more than one meaning of a word to determine the meaning that is funny.

---

18 Make Inferences   Name _____ Date _____

To Go or Not to Go

Read the science fiction story.
Then follow the directions in the Text Marking box.

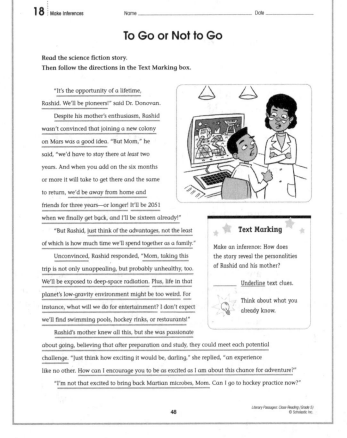

"It's the opportunity of a lifetime, Rashid. We'll be pioneers!" said Dr. Donovan.

Despite his mother's enthusiasm, Rashid wasn't convinced that joining a new colony on Mars was a good idea. "But Mom," he said, "we'd have to stay there at least two years. And when you add on the six months or more it will take to get there and the same to return, we'd be away from home and friends for three years—or longer! It'll be 2051 when we finally get back, and I'll be sixteen already!"

"But Rashid, just think of the advantages, not the least of which is how much time we'll spend together as a family."

Unconvinced, Rashid responded, "Mom, taking this trip is not only unappealing, but probably unhealthy, too. We'll be exposed to deep-space radiation. Plus, life in that planet's low-gravity environment might be too weird. For instance, what will we do for entertainment? I don't expect we'll find swimming pools, hockey rinks, or restaurants!"

Rashid's mother knew all this, but she was passionate about going, believing that after preparation and study, they could meet each potential challenge. "Just think how exciting it would be, darling," she replied, "an experience like no other. How can I encourage you to be as excited as I am about this chance for adventure?"

"I'm not that excited to bring back Martian microbes, Mom. Can I go to hockey practice now?"

Text Marking

Make an inference: How does the story reveal the personalities of Rashid and his mother?

_____ Underline text clues.

💡 Think about what you already know.

48

Literary Passages: Close Reading (Grade 5)
© Scholastic Inc.

Passage 18: To Go or Not to Go

1. D; Sample answer: I picked D because I think the expression refers to something so unusual, unique, and possibly life-changing, it doesn't happen very often.

2. C; Sample answer: I picked C because that word is used in paragraph 5, and also, her conversation with Rashid shows that she really wants this adventure.

3. Sample answer: Rashid seems like a smart, informed, but skeptical person who isn't convinced that this adventure is worth the risks and problems he foresees. On the other hand, his mother, while also smart and informed, seems fearless and more adventurous.

4. Sample answer: First of all, it's set in the future—2048 to be exact. It discusses a possible settlement on Mars, which is not yet possible, though it may happen one day.

Egg of Chaos

Read the Chinese creation myth.
Then follow the directions in the Text Marking box.

At first, the universe was jumbled inside a huge egg. That murky chaos contained all forms of opposites, or *yin* and *yang*. In the whirling mixture were water and fire, night and day, north and south, and so on. And there was Pangu, the being who would one day create our world.

Pangu slept inside the egg of chaos for 18,000 years. During that time, the *yin* and *yang* of all things was tangled together. He separated the heavier *yin* from the lighter *yang*. The *yang* floated up to become the sky while the *yin* settled to become the earth.

Standing between the two parts, Pangu's head touched sky and his feet strode upon earth. Over the next 18,000 years, sky and earth grew ever more vast, moving apart by ten feet each day.

Pangu also grew, keeping sky and earth separated. By the time of his death, earth and sky had settled into their places. One of Pangu's eyes became the sun, the other the moon. His breath became wind and clouds; his voice turned into the sound of thunder. Pangu's body formed great mountains and his blood its flowing waters. His veins became roads and his muscles fertile fields. His hairs remained in the sky as glittering stars.

Text Marking

Summarize the story.

⬭   Circle the main idea of the story.

____   Underline important details.

Literary Passages: Close Reading (Grade 5)
© Scholastic Inc.

⬤ Sample Text Markings

Passage 19: Egg of Chaos

1. C; Sample answer: I picked C because the author explains this in the second sentence of the piece.

2. B; Sample answer: I picked B because in the third and fourth paragraphs, the myth explains the cause of this separation.

3. Sample answer: Health and sickness are opposites but related like *yin* and *yang*. Health is being well, while sickness is its opposite—lack of health. One hopes to stay healthy, but sickness can rob one's health at any time.

4. Sample answer: The being Pangu grew inside the egg of chaos for 18,000 years, along with all the *yin* and *yang* of the universe. When he broke out of the egg, *yin* and *yang* formed earth and sky. When he died, parts of his body turned into parts of earth and sky.

Febold Feboldson's Find

Read the tall tale from the American Midwest.
Then follow the directions in the Text Marking box.

You've probably tasted the popular American popcorn ball. You might imagine some cook thinking to use syrup to stick popcorn together into a tasty snack. Well, that's NOT how popcorn balls came to be, at least according to old Febold Feboldson. He claimed that the popcorn ball invented itself during the weird summer of 1874.

Midwestern farmers called that growing season The Year of Striped Weather. That's because it alternated rainy and hot, not day by day, but by sections of cropland. Fields grew in stripes: first you'd see a mile-wide stripe of crops wilting in the broiling heat, then a mile-wide stripe of waterlogged crops soaking nearly to death.

Febold Feboldson had this situation on his farm. He grew corn in the Dismal River valley and sugar cane on the hills above. One day the sun baked his corn plants so hot that the kernels popped, causing a yellow blizzard. Meanwhile, the rain was drenching his sugar cane stalks so badly that the syrup inside washed out and rolled toward the popcorn. A ball soon formed, growing gigantic as it tumbled along. Febold estimated the giant popcorn ball at about two hundred feet wide!

His neighbor, Bert Bergstrom, witnessed this eye-popping event. Bert offered to help Febold corral the great popcorn ball to impress visitors. But just then, a swarm of hungry grasshoppers devoured the entire very-first popcorn ball.

Text Marking

Summarize the story.
Think about its theme.

⬭   Circle the main idea of the story.

____   Underline important details.

Literary Passages: Close Reading (Grade 5)
© Scholastic Inc.

⬤ Sample Text Markings

Passage 20: Febold Feboldson's Find

1. A; Sample answer: I picked A because it is the most sensible answer, based on the story.

2. C; Sample answer: I picked C because the other three words are synonyms for being very wet.

3. Sample answer: Febold Feboldson's crops grew in such a way that, during the Year of Striped Weather, the popcorn ball invented itself, and he found the first one ever on his farm.

4. Sample answer: I think that since this is a tall tale, the whole idea of the popcorn ball inventing itself is outlandish. Then, to have it devoured means there's no proof that it ever existed, except as a wild yarn.

Notes